Time Management for Attorneys:

A Lawyer's Guide to Decreasing Stress, Eliminating Interruptions & Getting Home on Time

Mark Powers and Shawn McNalis

Cover design by Leanne Thomas

ISBN: 978-0-615-18745-7

12 11 10 09 08 5 4 3 2

Contents

About the Authors

Mark Powers, president of Atticus, has been coaching attorneys on practice management and marketing for nearly 20 years. An international speaker, Mark has coached thousands of attorneys in his work with the Law Society of Scotland, the American Bar Association, and bar associations in Arizona, Florida, Massachusetts, Mississippi, New York, Connecticut, South Carolina, Texas, and the Midwest. Mark also conducts a program titled "Rainmakers" for attorneys across the country who wish to build client-development skills and a boot camp–style program called the "Practice Builder" for solo, small, and mid-size firm practitioners. In addition, he leads troubleshooting retreats that deal with partnership issues, difficult retirement scenarios, client development, and productivity problems. Mark is known for his expert advice on legal marketing, and in 1995 he co-authored *The Making of a Rainmaker: An Ethical Approach to Marketing for Solo and Small Firm Practitioners*, published by the Florida Bar. He has been featured in publications such as *Lawyers Weekly USA, Money* magazine, *Journal of the American Bar Association, Journal of the Law Society of Scotland, Florida Bar News,* and *Massachusetts Bar Association Lawyers Journal*, among many others. Prior to beginning work with the legal profession, Mark served as the chief executive officer and president of a multimillion-dollar, privately held company and as a corporate manager in a *Fortune* 500 company based in Connecticut. A native of Massachusetts, he has a master's degree from Northeastern University. His undergraduate studies include bachelor's degrees in economics and criminal justice.

Shawn McNalis is a former Imagineer with the Walt Disney Company and credits her 15-year career with Disney for her creative, collaborative approach to advising attorneys. In partnership with Mark Powers for 12 years, Shawn is a senior practice advisor and trainer for Atticus and co-authored *The Making of a Rainmaker,* commissioned and published by the Florida Bar in 1995. A former columnist for the *Massachusetts Lawyer's Weekly* and a faculty member of the Massachusetts Bar Association Institute in 1998, Shawn has authored and co-authored numerous articles on law practice management that have appeared in the ABA's *Law Practice Management Magazine*, *Journal of the*

Association of Legal Administrators, *ABA Family Law Section Magazine*, *The Florida Bar News*, *The Lawyer's Competitive Edge*, *The Florida Bar Workers Compensation Section Journal*, and *Massachusetts Bar Journal*, among many others. Frequently quoted in *Lawyer's Weekly USA* and past coach for the Orlando *Sentinel*'s "Career Makeover" column, she was a contributing author for the *Association of Legal Administrators Online Encyclopedia*, published in 2002. Shawn has been a featured speaker at meetings of the Law Society of Scotland, the New York State Bar Association, the Florida Bar Association, the Massachusetts Bar Association, the South Carolina Bar, and the 2003 Coaching Convention in Tokyo.

Preface

Our mission at Atticus is to keep our attorney clients focused on what is really important in life, to provide the training and skills necessary to build and maintain a sustainable practice, and to provide a structure of accountability and support for goal achievement.

Atticus was founded in 1989 to provide in-depth, ongoing support and accountability programs for lawyers and law firms that will effectively accomplish the following:

- Increase gross revenues and personal incomes
- Reduce stress and the number of hours in the office
- Develop greater career satisfaction
- Allow more time for family and personal interests

When first we began working with attorneys, we were focused on helping them to develop new business. It was our belief then, and still is, that without new business coming through the door on a regular basis, a law practice will not survive. We found our ideas to be well received. Everyone accepted that developing new business was a crucial skill, but as it turned out, it seemed to be a difficult task for our attorney clients to accomplish. Believing we were focused on the greatest area of need, we persisted in teaching seminars and advising our attorney clients on developing their business, or, as we say, developing clients. Along the way we discovered that in fact there was a need much greater than client development, and until this need was filled, no other need could be resolved.

Although our clients enthusiastically embraced our ideas on client development, they would repeatedly complain that they did not have time to implement the strategies and techniques provided in our seminars and coaching sessions. The attorneys knew they needed new business, and they worried about their current client list being too small. Despite all this, they did not believe they had the time to spend on client development. Initially, we regarded their failure to take consistent action as a form of resistance. Going out and developing new clients carries with it some risk of rejection, and it is natural to be hesitant at first. However, the inability to take action seemed to run deeper.

Upon further investigation, we discovered that many attorneys have no time for client development because they don't know how to *make* the time. Even if they were willing to implement new client development strategies, they were rendered incapable by their inability to get organized and manage themselves and their time. In spite of their outward appearance, many otherwise highly skilled practitioners are adrift in the sea of chaos that is their practice.

We found this to be especially true among small firm and solo practitioners. These very bright, well-respected individuals were overwhelmed by the combination of their legal work and the managerial duties that came with being an owner or a partner. They were so overwhelmed that they felt they couldn't effectively integrate any new skill, however much they desired it.

Not only did they not have any education in how to manage their time in the practice of law, they believed the task to be next to impossible. They had come to think of the law office as a place that was *inherently* chaotic and crisis-driven. They were convinced to the degree that if they hadn't already learned it, there was no training out there that would meet their needs.

They were right in the sense that time management skills are not taught in law school. Historically, the best way to learn about time management was to be lucky enough to be mentored by, or at least exposed to, someone who could manage his or her time well. If you had a good model, you learned from him or her. If not, you worked away with increasing inefficiency. Unfortunately for most people, working inefficiently leads to a lot of frustration and a constant feeling of being out of control.

In an effort to help clients regain a sense of control over their practices, we began to develop a time management curriculum specifically tailored to the law office. We pulled what good advice we could from a broad range of time management studies. These ranged from philosophies that were beautifully simplistic but light on implementation to those designed for improving production-line efficiencies. None of these approaches worked in totality because the law office is a unique environment. Fortunately, at the time, we were working with many generous clients who acted as willing guinea pigs in formulating the right approach.

A pivotal conversation occurred shortly after we began our search for solutions. In a coaching conversation with an attorney in Tallahassee, Florida, we began discussing the typical types of tasks that he undertook on a regular basis. To him, the number and types of tasks seemed limitless. In an effort to distinguish them and make sense of it all, we divided them up according to when they would occur. We started with his year and discussed the tasks and activities that occurred annually. This list included items such as end-year partnership bonus calculations, the firm's holiday open house, and the fishing trip he took every summer. We then looked at tasks that occurred on a quarterly and a monthly basis, such as quarterly filing of taxes and the monthly partners' meeting. We continued to make task lists for weekly events and, finally, daily events.

A pattern began to emerge. His days, weeks, months, and years were filled with tasks and activities that could be predicted and those that could not. We discovered that this was a clue to understanding the mystery of law practice time management and the high degree of anxiety surrounding it.

We saw that if we could create a format for standing blocks of time to accommodate the commonly recurring, predictable tasks, these would serve as the dependable "anchors" in the attorney's calendar. These anchors were in the "must do" category, and by scheduling them first, his calendar became more stable. Unfortunately, there were still the less-predictable tasks to deal with. We looked at how we could design the ideal week and the ideal day to help him handle the predictable tasks and yet be flexible enough to handle the unpredictable tasks that would come up on demand.

It was around those early coaching conversations that we built our primitive concepts of what we call the **time template**. With the input over the years of hundreds of other attorneys, we have refined our time management techniques to include training on managing interruptions, the fine art of delegation, client selection, and so on. The time template remains the centerpiece of each.

We realize that no one can ever control 100% of their time, but a good 75% to 80% of your time can be more predictable if you implement the time management tools and strategies provided in this book. Complete the Exercises designed to help you manage your time more effectively and study and adapt the Examples we have included, both of which are located in the book and on the accompanying CD-ROM. Implement the practice-specific forms also included on CD-ROM as part of your daily practice. When we speak of your life, we mean your life as a lawyer and as an individual. A law practice and a personal life don't have to be mutually exclusive. It really is possible to have a practice that serves your life instead of enslaving you.

Acknowledgments

Special thanks to Mark Chinn, a member of the American Bar Association's Section of Family Law Publications Board, who initially posed the idea of turning our Atticus seminar materials into a book. We appreciate his ongoing faith in our programs.

Thanks to Hilda Spain-Owen for her outstanding ability to grasp concepts quickly and organize them into logical sequences. She was an invaluable member of the Atticus team and served as a coach in many areas of book writing.

Also appreciated are the many attorneys we have worked with over the last several years who contributed to this book on many levels.

We also gratefully acknowledge J.R. Phelps and the Florida Bar for contributing several administrative forms to this book and for his friendship and support of Atticus over the years. Thanks also to Cynthia Swanson for contributing her internal checklists, Richard West, Caroline Black, Pilot George Patrick Owen, Doug Sealey, and Harriett Steinberg for sharing their wealth of experience and hard-earned wisdom.

We also acknowledge and appreciate the contributions and dedication of the Atticus Practice Advisors, Patrick Wilson, Glenn Gutek, Cammie Hauser, Glenn Finch, Nora Bergman, Judi Craig and Vinnie Bonazzoli.

Many thanks also to Molly McCormick for her editing help with the second draft and Carole Warshaw for her excellent proofreading and copyediting of the final draft.

Introduction

Two Approaches to Time Management: Reactive and Proactive

Attorneys tend to approach time management either by passively responding to the demands placed upon them by their environment or by proactively creating their environment. We call these two approaches the **reactive style** and the **proactive style.**

The Reactive Style of Time Management

Those who believe they cannot control their lives or feel that they are at the mercy of circumstances are operating in the reactive style. If you arrive at your office in the morning fully expecting to make great strides on one or two important cases only to be interrupted by urgent requests from clients in crisis or staff demanding your attention, you understand the lure of the reactive mode of operating. If you succumb, however, you end most days wondering where the time went, as the important cases you intended to work on are now buried beneath all the other files that you hastily pulled during your firefighting efforts throughout the day. You suddenly must choose whether to work on the untouched files now, at 6:00 p.m., or work over the weekend and miss your child's soccer game or dance recital, or your fishing trip that you continue to postpone because you have to play catch-up on the weekends.

The reactive style of operating is a short-term way of thinking, not tied to a larger vision or mission. Attorneys who labor under this method often feel that things are out of control and approach the world with "learned helplessness." Usually, they've given up even trying to control their circumstances. People will give up the effort to exert some order upon their universe when they've decided they can't effect a change. These attorneys are doomed to always work for someone else's agenda—to fulfill someone else's goals, not their own.

To see if you qualify as one who labors under the reactive style, look at Exercise I-1, The Reactive Style Checklist. Chances are good that if you check off more than three items, you are behaving reactively.

EXERCISE I-1: THE REACTIVE STYLE CHECKLIST

Instructions: Read through the list of behaviors associated with the reactive style. Check off those that apply to you.

- ❑ Operating with a survival mentality—not working toward a long-term vision for your practice; focusing only on how you will make it through the day, the week and the month
- ❑ Not marketing your practice with any consistency
- ❑ Constantly handling client crises—doing a lot of damage control and never feeling like you have the time to do your best work
- ❑ Generating income but not producing a real profit
- ❑ Practicing threshold law—working with undesirable clients out of fear that you have to take any business that "crosses your threshold"
- ❑ Delegating very little—either out of a general distrust for the work of others or because you haven't anyone to whom you can delegate
- ❑ Burning out and/or considering getting out of your area of law altogether

The Hazards of the Reactive Style

The ability to react to circumstances is a highly valued skill. However, it becomes a problem when those circumstances change at a faster and faster rate. If your only plan is to react, you fall into the trap of rating your productivity only on your speed and level of "busyness." In truth, you are doing nothing more than reacting to the rhythm of the forces around you. Before too long, you become addicted to this "busyness" through the adrenaline rush that has enabled you to keep your head barely above water.

Our ability to release adrenaline into our system in order to run faster or fight harder has been essential to our survival as a species. Countless generations of human beings have relied upon the "fight or flight" instinct when in danger. It is our *emergency* energizing system. It is not intended to be used every day, all day long, to help us cope with daily life. However, it is the push many attorneys rely on every day to get the job done. There is a high cost associated with this mode of operation. Medical studies show an important link between the hormone cortisol, triggered by adrenaline release, and heart disease. If your style of time management is reactive, you pay a high price for the bursts of energy you may have come to depend upon—and you are not alone.

"They always say that time changes things, but you actually have to change them yourself."
—Andy Warhol

Attorneys from all over the world report that they rely upon their adrenaline to kick in and carry them through crisis situations. After making that revelation, they promptly describe their law practice as "one crisis after another." Universally speaking, any appearance in court, let alone a trial of any kind, tends to be accompanied by a significant boost of adrenaline. This boost enhances initial energy and then leaves attorneys drained when they walk out of the courtroom. In fact, one of the symptoms of excessive reliance on adrenaline is that without a pending deadline, you are not motivated to lift a finger. Even typically overachieving attorneys report to us that they find themselves sitting numbly behind their desks the day after a trial, unable to motivate themselves to do anything. When their adrenaline stores are drained, they sit without a clue as to why they can't function at their normal speed.

Moving Away from the Reactive Style

There are steps you can take to move away from the reactive style of time management. If you think that you may be a candidate, you can begin by tuning in when you feel the adrenaline start to flow. That's when you need to look around and see what's triggering it. Following are some guidelines for going through that process and how to take action to move toward proactivity.

Notice When You Are Running on an Adrenaline Boost

The only way to overcome a cycle of constant reaction and the accompanying adrenaline addiction is to begin monitoring your own behavior. Step one is to notice when you are running on adrenaline. At best, during the boost, you may feel highly motivated; at worst, you may feel fretful, anxious, or even panicky. Your heart may be beating faster than normal and you may take quicker, shallower breaths. You may feel very restless, have a hard time focusing on one thing, and feel compelled to work on many things at once, as everything seems equally important. Attention to detail is difficult at this point. Mentally, you may be saying to yourself things like:

- I'll never have enough time to finish this.
- Why did I wait so long to start this?
- I hope I make it to court on time.

These are all the behavioral and mental symptoms of an adrenaline push.

Analyze the Situation

When you are in such a state, it is time to stop and analyze the situation. More than likely you will find yourself suffering from a shortage, or a perception of a shortage, in one or more of these three areas:

- Time
- Money (cash flow or financial security)
- Energy (your personal energy or availability of manpower to assist you)

If you experience a feeling of abundance in the areas of time, money and/or energy, your mind would not constantly be shifting your body into overdrive. When most stressors are traced back to their roots, it is a shortage in one of these three areas that is responsible.

Symptoms of a Time Shortage Perception

When you notice an adrenaline rush and your analysis of the situation points to *time* as the area in which you feel therc is a lack, you probably can relate to the following:

- Always feel pressed for time
- Run a half-hour to an hour behind
- Say "yes" to many more tasks, appointments, and meetings than you can complete
- Have no daily or weekly plans
- Wonder why others seem to be achieving more
- Close associates and friends always expect you to be late

Think of this as "hurry sickness." Attorneys are especially susceptible to this predicament because of the highly charged nature of their work as problem solvers. Even when your day is well scheduled, it can rapidly deteriorate when a client has a crisis. By the time the second client crisis hits, your planned activities are now either compressed into the rest of your day or you work late (or the weekend) to make up the time taken up by the crises. The sense that there is not enough time to handle everything is the number one reason that lawyers rely so heavily on adrenaline.

Symptoms of a Money Shortage Consciousness

When you notice an adrenaline rush and your analysis of the situation points to *money* as the area in which you feel there is a lack, you might:

- Accept clients that are outside normal standards because you need the income;
- Disregard risk of liability or not getting paid if even a promise of income is present;
- Remain with law partners despite waning compatibility simply for financial security; or
- Practice in an area of law because it pays well even though the passion is not there.

There are innumerable ways in which a lack of money will add to the stress, the adrenaline rush, and the subsequent adrenaline addiction. In a law practice, the lack of money will most often lead to practicing "threshold law"—working with clients who have unreasonable expectations, who desire revenge, or who present some other situation that the law is not designed to handle. This is often the client who does not respect you and may be unable to pay in the end. In addition, unpleasant and uncooperative clients can be very demanding, which can lead to time crises in other areas of your professional and personal life. You are then forced into overdrive, and the adrenaline addiction increases its hold.

Symptoms of an Energy Shortage Consciousness

When you notice an adrenaline rush and your analysis of the situation points to energy as the area in which you feel you are lacking, you probably can relate to the following:

- Feel burned out and drained by dealing with difficult clients
- Work long hours and feel unable to function as well as you used to
- Sense of humor may have disappeared
- Find no pleasure in helping clients and often resent them
- Painfully aware of no one to delegate work to if working as a solo practitioner with little or no staff support

Whether the problem is a shortage of personal energy or no one to help you, you may be dealing with a chronic lack of energy, which can be very debilitating.

Take Action

Once you've figured out that you're operating in the reactive style of management, you have the opportunity to move beyond the behaviors that have kept you there. The key to moving beyond this destructive style is to take action by trying new proactive behaviors.

The Proactive Style of Time Management

When a lawyer exhibits the proactive style, he or she uses tools and implements strategies to choose behaviors that *create* desirable circumstances in both his or her personal and professional lives. They are the designers of their circumstances, not the victims.

These attorneys have taken the view that time management is actually self-management. This is the style exhibited by those who take responsibility for their time and how they spend it. They stop, take stock, and set goals for themselves so they won't be constantly buffeted by events or thrown off track. These are the attorneys who set themselves up to succeed by measuring the results they achieve financially. They know that it is important for clients to have accessibility and to feel taken care of by the law office. Each of these attorneys is careful about client selection. Each creates systems to preempt crisis and takes a team approach to client care. Absent is the sense of helplessness and resignation that characterizes the reactive attorney. They are not victimized by their practice. In this style, the truly important issues are not sacrificed for the seemingly urgent day-to-day issues that may not make a difference in the long run. For this group, the business of the law office is as interesting as the practice itself.

One way these lawyers hit the high mark when it comes to maintaining a proactive style of time management is to monitor themselves. Use Exercise I-2, The Proactive Style Checklist, to give you an idea of your level of proactive time management skills. When you are able to check more than three boxes, chances are good that you are beginning to take control of your practice. We have seen over and over that it is possible to lead a successful practice, one that makes sustainable profits and allows you to have a satisfying personal life.

EXERCISE I-2: THE PROACTIVE STYLE CHECKLIST

Instructions: Read through the list of behaviors typical of the proactive style. Check those that apply to you.

- ❑ The entrepreneurial mentality (working toward a long-term vision for your practice)
- ❑ Always marketing referral sources to cultivate future business
- ❑ Creating a "crisis-free" zone in your firm by systemizing and exercising preventive measures
- ❑ Producing profit and building a strong financial foundation
- ❑ Building your reputation by working with desirable clients
- ❑ Delegating to associates, paralegals or legal secretaries for maximum efficiency and profitability
- ❑ Experiencing satisfaction with your practice and feeling that it supports your personal life

Set Up Boundaries

On the road toward the proactive style, the first thing you want to do is set up boundaries to protect you from yourself. As you may have sometimes suspected, you are often your own worst enemy. The boundaries you set up for yourself can be thought of as your personal parameters, designed not to limit your behaviors in a negative way but to create a healthier way of operating for the long term.

Below are some examples of boundaries as personal parameters. They are broken down conveniently in the areas in which most attorneys feel the biggest pinch: time, money, and energy. Feel free to borrow, modify, eliminate, and add to the list in order to assemble healthy parameters of your own.

- **If you feel you don't have enough time**, consider adopting some or all of these boundaries when you are setting up your schedule.

  - Not working past 6:00 p.m.
  - Not working on weekends

- No more than two evenings out during the week
- No interruptions during production time at the office
- Cleaning your desk at the end of each day
- Preparing for important deadlines, legal or otherwise, well in advance of the date
- Creating private "retreat" days to proactively plan for your professional future
- Arriving home before dinner is on the table
- Arriving home before the kids go to bed
- Creating a "date night" with your significant other
- Planning weekly family nights
- Taking the kids to school in the morning
- Planning a yearly vacation of two weeks in a row

- **If you feel you don't have enough money**, consider adopting some or all of these boundaries when you are setting up your schedule.

    - Engaging only in work that is profitable for you
    - Requiring a retainer prior to beginning work with a client
    - Systemizing your bookkeeping practices by creating a monthly template for all of your recurring financial tasks
    - Hiring a trained bookkeeper to assist with your accounting
    - Creating and maintaining a reserve account as an emergency cushion
    - Using a financial team that you trust
    - Monitoring the financial status of your files consistently to ensure that you are being paid

- **If you feel you don't have enough energy**, consider adopting some or all of these boundaries when you are setting up your schedule.

    - Being very selective and not working with high-maintenance or difficult clients
    - Eating lunch every day to support your energy level
    - Establishing daily closed-door production time to handle your highest-priority work
    - Arriving at the office early if you are most energetic in the morning

- Leveraging yourself by hiring competent staff members to whom you can delegate tasks
- Exercising a minimum of three times per week to reduce stress and stay physically and mentally balanced

Without these or your own particular boundaries in place, you may find it easy to slip back into the reactive mode of operating. You are constantly bombarded with demands that range from the unimportant to crisis-level firefighting. Having these boundaries in place and committing to them faithfully gives you and those around you a sense of stability and a foundation upon which to build a high-performing practice.

Implement the Proactive Approach

Once you've mentally resolved to adopt your new boundaries, go public with those around you. Let your family or spouse know you'll be coming home earlier. Tell your partner or office staff you'll no longer work with questionable clients and ask for their support. We coach many attorneys to enlist the aid of their partners and staff and the help they provide is invaluable. Some attorneys we work with actually have a small committee that approves all new clients upon intake to support the principle in not taking on inappropriate clients. You may engage your bookkeeper, office manager or partner's assistance in adopting new financial boundaries. They can assist in systemizing bookkeeping tasks, starting a reserve account and making it a policy to require retainers. Our clients submit to this kind of rigorous support because they know it's easy to slip back to their old habits. If asked, you can bet your family, friends and co-workers will remind you of your promises. Your job is to accept their intervention and not override their support.

The remaining chapters in this book will provide you with further distinctions in the area of time management, but taking a proactive stance is critical to implementing every single time management strategy we discuss in this book. In order to take control of your practice, you must change your behaviors. And to change your behaviors, you must step out of your comfort zone and be proactive.

Chapter 1

Proactive Strategy One: Create a Personal Vision Statement

If you are committed to the boundaries you have set for yourself, you have taken a giant step toward ensuring that you will manage your time. Now it's time to add some strategies to your arsenal that will support your efforts to achieve a higher level of proactivity. In this chapter, we will discuss the purpose of a personal vision statement, give you instructions on how to create one, and show you examples of vision statements from others in your field.

Writing a personal vision statement allows you to do two things:

1. Outline what you value, and
2. Design a plan to include what you value in a life you deem worth living.

Michael Gerber, author of *The E-Myth Revisited,* calls this statement your "primary aim," and Steven Covey, author of *The Seven Habits of Highly Effective People*, calls it your "personal mission statement." It is up to you to write the script, assemble the plot, and decide on the main characters. Once you've done that, your job is to "live into it." If this seems laborious, realize that you are now living your life without a plan. You could compare that to going on a vacation without a plan, which you probably wouldn't even consider. Before you begin establishing a plan to make your business more successful, it's important to discover *why* that goal is important to you. The answer to the "why" question can be found by focusing on your personal vision first.

Many, if not most, of the struggles, challenges, and triumphs in your daily life involve your career. However, you must ensure that your career is serving your personal vision and not the other way around. Building your practice will continue to be a struggle for you unless you see how it serves your personal aims. If you look at this as "one more thing to do," you will defeat the purpose.

Clarify Your Core Values

To assist you in creating your personal vision statement, we have designed a worksheet to help you decide what is important to you and how satisfied you are with the way you currently incorporate these life elements. Complete Exercise 1-1, Values Clarification Worksheet.

EXERCISE 1-1: VALUES CLARIFICATION WORKSHEET

Instructions: Read through the list of life elements and rate them in each column as instructed.

What Matters Most to You?

Below are eight common life elements. In the first column, list them in the order that best demonstrates how much you value each. If you value "family" the most, then write "family" on line one. In the second column, rate your level of satisfaction with how well you are managing this element of your life. For example, if you wrote "family" in the first column on line one and you think you are doing a moderate job in that area, write the number "2" in column two.

When you complete the ranking, compare the satisfaction rating you gave to each core value with that core value's order of importance. Ideally, your most highly placed values all rate a high satisfaction level.

Family	Work	Health	Personal Development
Spirituality	Recreation	Socializing	Financial Planning/Thinking

Level of Importance: Rank: 1 High – 8 Low	**Level of Satisfaction:** Score: 1 High – 2 Medium – 3 Low
1.	
2.	
3.	
4.	
5.	
6.	
7.	
8.	

Now that you have rated an array of core values and how well you think you are managing what you value, Exercise 1-2 will help you explore the amount of time you spend on each of those elements.

EXERCISE 1-2: WHERE DOES THE TIME GO?

Instructions: Draw a picture and indicate the percentages that represent the amount of time you spend in the following areas: Family, Work, Socializing, Personal Development, Spirituality, Recreation, Financial Planning/Thinking, Health.

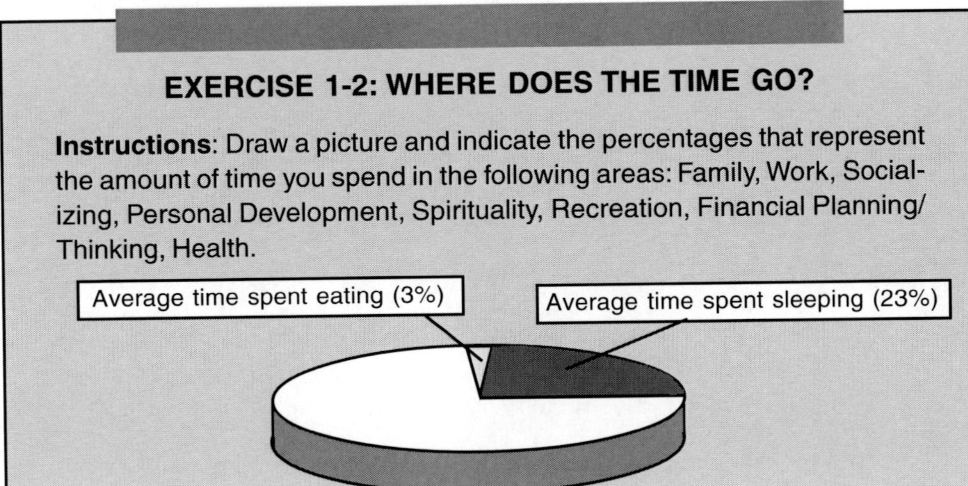

Begin Your Personal Vision Statement

You have been guided through a thought process that has given you some solid information. Use this information as you complete Exercise 1-3, Beginning Your Personal Vision Statement.

EXERCISE 1-3: BEGINNING YOUR PERSONAL VISION STATEMENT

Instructions: Read through the incomplete sentences and the suggested endings that accompany them in parentheses. Complete the sentences using our suggestions or simply create your own. Whatever you do, it should be an accurate reflection of what you envision for yourself.

1. In my family life I am committed to

   ____

   ____

   (spending time with, enjoying, teaching, working with, taking care of, etc.) my

   ____

   ____

   (spouse, significant other, friends, family and/or children).

2. For recreation I enjoy (will spend time)

   ____

   ____

   (reading, fine dining, skiing, martial arts, tennis, golf, etc.)

3. My home environment will be

____

____

(nurturing, comfortable, a place for entertainment, on the water, spacious, equipped with a home office . . .)

4. My retirement home will be

____

____

(a cabin in the mountains, a seaside condominium, a small restored Victorian home, a large, spacious home designed to accommodate visiting grandchildren and guests. . .).

5. For (hobbies, passions, interests), I enjoy (will spend time on)

____

____

6. I will maintain (or regain) my health by

____

____

(exercising, eating healthy foods, lowering my stress level, getting adequate rest . . .).

Use the Personal Vision Statements of Others to Guide You

Below are some examples of personal visions. As you can see, they range in style from the practical to the poetic. They distinctly reflect their authors' personalities in style and approach.

EXAMPLE 1-1: PERSONAL VISION STATEMENTS

Personal Vision Example 1

In my life I am committed to loving my spouse and raising my three children in a secure environment filled with love, encouragement, and fun. I will achieve this by providing them with abundant educational opportunities to learn about the world around them, giving them a foundation of trust, and supporting their growth by spending time with them exploring their unique talents and gifts.

My home will be a comfortable and nurturing place for myself, my spouse and the children.

It will be both a refuge from the world and a place to have fun and entertain friends. It will be large, spacious and impeccably clean. It will be a warm and inviting environment for our individual hobbies, interests and family activities.

I will practice wisdom in maintaining my health and will guide my family to do the same for themselves. Exercise will always be an important element in our lifestyle. We will watch our diet on an ongoing basis and value rest and relaxation to provide a balance to our busy lives.

Our law firm will provide superior-quality legal service to best serve the needs of our clients. We will achieve this by positioning our firm to attract a staff devoted to providing excellent service in the area of estate planning. Integrity will continue to be our watchword as we grow not only in size but in scope of services. We will never grow so big, however, that we lose touch with our commitments and forget that our clients are the reason we are in business. Our leadership in the area of estate planning will gain us a solid reputation not only in our local community but across the state and will lead to prosperity in both wealth and personal satisfaction.

Personal Vision Example 2

I will devote part of my life to taking care of my parents, who are elderly. I will spend a great deal of my time with my spouse, and also my grown children and grandchildren when they come to visit. In the rest of my free time I will work with my husband to remodel and restore old houses, as this is something we both enjoy. When I am in my mid-sixties and retired, we hope to move into an old, lakeside Victorian home we have restored.

My law practice will thrive and double in size before I retire. I will gain a partner and additional staff to round out my ability to do commercial real estate and corporate law. I will be able to be out of the office one or two days out of the week, confident the business will run smoothly. I will acquire a small, freestanding office building, which will become my permanent location. I will earn enough to be financially independent and free of debt by age sixty. I will have a substantial investment portfolio of nearly one million dollars by the year 2006.

We have worked with many different attorneys over the years, all with their own strengths and weaknesses. We have encouraged them to articulate their personal vision and to describe how their practice fits within and serves their life. We will now make the same request of you.

No two personal visions will look or sound alike. Allow yourself to create—to put pen to paper and actually write your life. It is a very powerful first step in achieving what you want. *Remember, this is not about* how *your vision will be accomplished, but an articulation of* what *your vision is.* You may choose to never show your personal vision to anyone or to keep it accessible and on display where you can see it often. You may involve your entire family. This team approach, whether it's family, the team at the office, or both, is one that many of our clients have taken. Whatever approach you use is fine, as long as it inspires you every time you look at it.

You have been guided through a series of steps leading up to writing an in-depth personal vision statement. The information presented and the information you discovered about yourself will assist you in writing your first draft. We have provided you with space in Exercise 1-4, Complete Your Personal Vision Statement, to get started.

EXERCISE 1-4: COMPLETE YOUR PERSONAL VISION STATEMENT

Instructions: Using the information you have gathered about yourself in the preceding exercises, write your vision in paragraph form. Think of this as a rough draft; polish it in a second draft.

In my personal life I am committed to

____

____

____

____

____

____

____

____

____

____

____

____

We highly recommend this first strategy, "create a personal vision statement," as a critical part of transitioning from reactive to proactive time management. It is not possible to overestimate its importance. Can you already get a feel for how your practice would change if you set boundaries based on time, money, and energy and committed to fulfilling your personal vision? To indicate the importance of the role that your personal life plays in your practice, and the doors proactive time management can open for you, we have included an exercise to help you plan something that many attorneys haven't done for years. In chapter 9, you will find an exercise designed to help you *plan a vacation.*

Although these are beginning steps, they can have a dynamic impact on your daily life and your future. In the subsequent chapters, you will see how the strategies relating to your practice can add even more quality to your life.

Chapter 2

Proactive Strategy Two: Create a Professional Vision Statement

A statement expressing your personal vision speaks volumes about who you are and the direction of your life path. It is helpful to think of this as separate and distinct from your professional life. To address the area of what you do, we will move on to your **professional vision statement.** We will discuss the purpose of a professional vision statement, give you instructions on how to create one, and show you examples of vision statements from others in your field. The purpose of the professional vision statement is twofold:

- To serve as a reflection of your values
- To articulate the philosophical foundation for the professional service you provide

Over time, your practice area and the makeup of your firm may change. By having a professional vision statement, you can be proactive in deciding if those changes are right for you. Such a statement will help you keep the picture firmly in your mind and enable you to see day-to-day fluctuations for what they are. You are then less likely to become reactive.

Clarify Your Core Professional Values

To assist you in creating your professional vision statement, we have designed an exercise to help you decide what is important to you. Complete Exercise 2-1, Business Values Worksheet, and follow the instructions.

EXERCISE 2-1: BUSINESS VALUES WORKSHEET

Instructions: Read through the list of core business values and rate them in each column as instructed.

What Matters Most in Your Practice?

Below are seven core business values. In the first column, list them in the order that best demonstrates how much you value each. If you value "delivering high-quality work" most, then write "delivering high-quality work" on line 1. In the second column, rate your level of satisfaction with how well you are managing this element of your professional life. For example, if you wrote "delivering high-quality work" in the first column on line 1 and you think you are doing a moderate job in that area, write the number "2" in column two.

1. Delivering high-quality work
2. Working with clients you like
3. Being profitable
4. Having a systemized practice
5. Achieving proper life/work balance
6. Employing a great legal team/staff
7. Creating a professional legacy

When you complete the ranking, compare the satisfaction rating you gave to each core value with that value's order of importance. Ideally, your most highly placed values all rate a high satisfaction level.

Level of Importance: Rank 1 High – 7 Low	**Level of Satisfaction:** Score 1 High – 2 Medium – 3 Low
1.	
2.	
3.	
4.	
5.	
6.	
7.	

What do your scores show you? Are you experiencing low levels of satisfaction in the domains you consider most important?

Begin Your Professional Vision Statement

Use the following questions to help you format an outline for your professional vision statement. The suggested answers are included to help stimulate your thinking. Feel free to modify our answers or create your own.

EXERCISE 2-2: BEGINNING YOUR PROFESSIONAL VISION STATEMENT

Instructions: Read through the incomplete sentences and the suggested endings that accompany them in parentheses. Complete the sentences using our suggestions or simply create your own. Whatever you do, it should be an accurate reflection of what you envision for yourself professionally.

1. I will concentrate my practice in the areas of ____________________

   ____

   ____

   (fill in with the appropriate practice areas).

2. My office environment will be ____________________

   ____

   ____

   (spacious, comfortable, impressive, well organized, fully automated, designed with the client in mind, a showcase for my talents . . .).

3. My financial plans are to ____________________

   ____

   ____

   (earn a minimum of $ ___ per year, save enough to put my children through college, buy a new office building, leverage my investments to retire at age ___ with a yearly income of $___, allow for more travel, buy a retirement home on the lake . . .).

4. My business philosophy is one of ____________________

   ____

   ____

   (caring for my clients with integrity and leadership, dedication to serving my clients through a team approach, providing service that continually exceeds the expectations of my clients, being known nationwide for my expertise or mediation skills, serving my clients with a commitment to systemization, automation and teamwork, crafting individualized solutions for my clients, assisting my clients as they move through changes in their lives, being a model law firm in the area of _________ law . . .).

EXERCISE 2-3: COMPLETE YOUR PROFESSIONAL VISION STATEMENT

Instructions: Using the information you have gathered about yourself in the preceding exercises, write your vision in paragraph form. Think of this as a rough draft; polish it in a second draft.

____

____

____

____

____

____

____

____

____

____

____

____

Now that you have at least an outline of your professional vision statement, you are prepared to dig deeper into the time management issues in your practice. Many others in your field have gone through this process of composing a vision for themselves and their practice. Your commitment to following through with the statements you have made are going to be the deciding factor in your success. We have confidence, through our experience with attorneys, that all of your efforts to try to implement your vision—even if you don't manifest it perfectly—will bring you closer to a practice that serves you and your clients and doesn't enslave you.

Chapter 3

Proactive Strategy Three: Set Strategic Goals

Once you've written your personal and professional vision statements, you can take advantage of more tools and strategies to move you toward realizing those visions. Create "stepping-stones" to take you in small but effective increments to the reality of your ultimate vision. We call these stepping-stones *strategic goals*. In this chapter, we present guidelines about strategic goals and acquaint you with a system for achieving them. Think of this section as a proactive time management strategy in this sense: Your future is influencing your present.

Below are two examples in which you can see how setting strategic goals serves as a way of creating stepping-stones toward your vision. Notice that the strategic goals state a specific action (enroll, write, teach, tell) you will take.

The first example belongs to an attorney who stated that she wished to become a nationally known expert in the area of criminal law. Below are strategic goals she set for herself related to her vision.

Goal: I will become a nationally known expert in criminal law.

- Create a Web site that represents my views
- Write articles for law journals
- Write a book
- Teach seminars
- Represent high-profile clients
- Hire a public relations firm to gain media coverage

The second example belongs to an attorney whose professional vision statement included expanding his practice to include additional services.

Goal: I will expand my practice to include adoption services.

- Enroll in three seminars on adoption
- Originate one to four new adoption clients a month
- Tell my referral sources that I wish to offer this service
- Write articles on adoption for my local bar journal

"Vision without action is merely a dream. Action without vision just passes the time. Vision with action can change the world."
— Joel Arthur Barker

Lawyers report that breaking their larger goals down into these smaller steps is psychologically reassuring. All of a sudden a large vision is reduced to achievable tasks. You are setting yourself up for small wins. A life well lived is composed of many small wins in service to the larger goal.

Case Study
Time Management Issue: Goal Setting

Attorney: Richard West
State: Florida

In 1985, Richard West moved to Orlando from Houston, Texas, to open a second office for his father's law firm, an insurance defense practice. It took only six months for him to realize that this type of practice was not for him. Exploring other practice areas led him to attend the American Academy of Matrimonial Lawyers Institute in Tampa, Florida. He found matrimonial law much more to his liking and focused on transitioning his practice.

Inspired to set goals in a time management seminar, he decided "to become the best divorce lawyer in Orlando." When asked to come up with intermediate strategies that would support the achievement of his long-term goal, he decided to become involved in the family law section of the Orange County Bar and the Florida Bar, and ultimately achieve a fellowship in the American Academy of Matrimonial Lawyers.

In addition, he decided to become board-certified in marital and family law, publish articles in trade journals, and raise his profile through speaking engagements. Thus, the short-term or daily goals that would help him reach his ultimate goal included filing an application for board certification, learning the qualifications for becoming a Fellow of the American Academy, and joining the family law section of the Florida and Orange County Bar Associations.

Once Richard began to put the plan into effect, he vowed to do *at least one thing daily that would advance him toward his goal.* He ultimately became board-certified, became a member of the executive council of the family law section of the local bar, served as president of the American Academy of Matrimonial Lawyers, Florida Chapter, chaired the Orange County Bar Association, and, at the writing of this book, currently chairs the family law section of the Florida Bar.

Richard's Good Advice:
"I don't know if I've achieved my goal of 'becoming the best family lawyer in Orlando,' but it was simply by going through this exercise, writing out the goals and then following the plan, that I have the successful practice that I have today."

Adopt a System for Implementing Your Strategic Goals: The Goal Grid

Often our attorney clients set promising strategic goals but fail to accomplish them. A simple tool can improve the prospects for goal achievement. It is an easy system called the *goal grid.* The structured format of the goal grid enables you to:

- Break down your strategic goals into even smaller measurable chunks;
- List goals in an accessible, user-friendly format; and
- Project target dates for completion.

Look at the following completed goal grid example from an attorney whose professional vision is to be known nationally as an expert in matrimonial law.

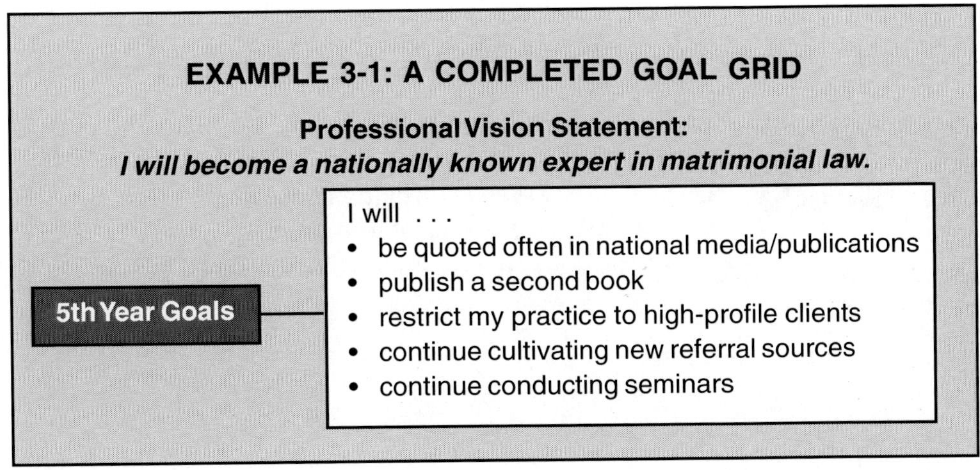

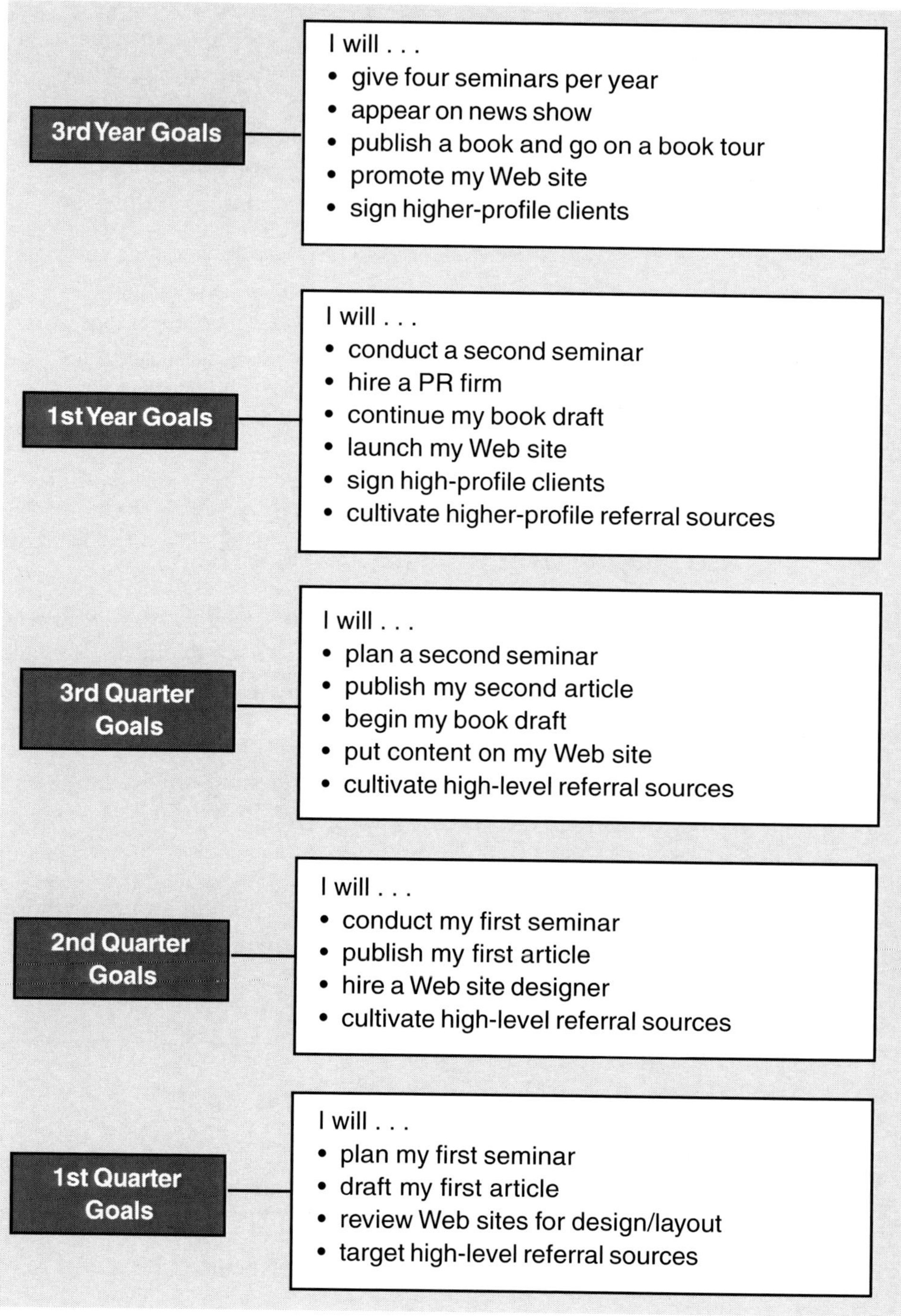
3rd Year Goals
I will . . .
• give four seminars per year
• appear on news show
• publish a book and go on a book tour
• promote my Web site
• sign higher-profile clients
1st Year Goals
I will . . .
• conduct a second seminar
• hire a PR firm
• continue my book draft
• launch my Web site
• sign high-profile clients
• cultivate higher-profile referral sources
3rd Quarter Goals
I will . . .
• plan a second seminar
• publish my second article
• begin my book draft
• put content on my Web site
• cultivate high-level referral sources
2nd Quarter Goals
I will . . .
• conduct my first seminar
• publish my first article
• hire a Web site designer
• cultivate high-level referral sources
1st Quarter Goals
I will . . .
• plan my first seminar
• draft my first article
• review Web sites for design/layout
• target high-level referral sources

This goal grid begins with one of the commitments from the attorney's vision statement. Notice that the large goal has been broken down into a series of small goals that are action-based (i.e., draft, cultivate, hire, plan) and attainable.

"The future does not get better by hope, it gets better by plan. And to plan for the future we need goals."
—Jim Rohn

This example is a typical design using five years as the projected final target date. It is divided into quarterly, then yearly, target dates. The first section is dedicated to quarterly goals for the next year, the second section for the first-year goals, the next for third-year goals, and finally for five-year goals. Listing these small strategic goals in the projected time slots is a critical element that can determine the success or failure of goal completion. A goal that does not have a deadline is a wish. Wishes are for those who avoid taking responsibility for creating their own futures. As the saying goes, "The best way to predict your future is to create it."

Create Your Own Goal Grid

After reviewing the sample goal grid, you probably have some ideas of your own to enter into a first draft of a goal grid. Complete Exercise 3-1 to get started on using this system to better accomplish your goals.

EXERCISE 3-1: CREATING YOUR OWN GOAL GRID

Instructions: Complete each of the following steps.

1. Select an ultimate goal from your professional vision statement and write it in the blank at the top of the grid.
2. Ask yourself what small actions you need to take to accomplish this ultimate goal. To get ideas, pretend you have already met the goal and imagine how your life would be different. Work backwards from there. Use these action words to help you brainstorm: **write, identify, build, hire, locate, create, and conduct.** Avoid words like **know, understand or appreciate.** They are too open to interpretation, too broad. As a test for an action-based strategic goal, ask yourself if you can actually see yourself performing the behavior.
3. List your strategic goals on the grid in the specified time slots for a five-year plan. Later you may want to design your own time line, but for your first draft, use the typical five-year plan.

Five-Year Goal Grid

Goal Statement: ____________________

5th Year Goals

3rd Year Goals

1st Year Goals

3rd Quarter Goals

2nd Quarter Goals

1st Quarter Goals

The goal grid system is an effective way to increase your chances of achieving your goals, large and small. The conditions you set in the form of weeks, months, and years give you a challenge—target dates—to work toward as opposed to dreaming the endless dream that you'll meet your goals. When you accomplish a strategic goal, see yourself as the winner you are.

"The innovator is someone who has the capacity not just of envisioning the future in an abstract, day-dreaming, fantasizing kind of way, but has the interest and the capability and the drive to actually do something about that vision."
—William Thompson

There is one more step you must take after you create the goal grid to make sure you enact the plan. Patrick Wilson, a senior practice advisor with Atticus, tells clients that these goals are worthless unless you apply the most powerful force in the universe: "ink on your calendar."

The final step is to put your strategic goals on your planner so you are proactively pursuing your vision, not just wishing it were so. You might also want to schedule some celebration time when you "win" one in the time management game.

Chapter 4

Proactive Strategy Four: Select Clients Wisely

In our effort to give you the strategies and tools to improve your time management, we want to bring to your attention that even the subtlest behaviors can sabotage your goal. You may be asking yourself, "How does the way I select my clients affect how much time I have to get my work done?" This chapter will answer that question and give you a system for client selection. We also identify ways that clients can be a drain on your time and eventually your well-being and, on the other hand, how they can be an asset to your practice.

Why Be So Selective?

If we were to apply Pareto's Principle, also known as the 80/20 Rule, to your client base, we would probably find that 80% of your income comes from 20% of your clients. Hidden among the clients that you serve, they are a small, quiet, but vitally important group. Studies show that this 20% of your clients who provide the most income have certain characteristics. If you can learn to recognize those characteristics, you can begin to target them as future clients and raise the percentage of your more profitable clients.

Before we introduce our system for selecting clients, we would like to touch on some of the factors that make it crucial for you to implement some plan for selectivity.

How to Tell the "Good" Clients From the "Bad"

The client selection task that faces attorneys is more difficult than that of many professionals due to the volatile nature of many clients and their disputes. Nice, normally well-grounded and cooperative individuals can engage in uncharacteristically extreme behavior during the course of your representation. It can be very difficult to tell the good clients from the bad when they are on an emotional roller-coaster.

Given the emotional state of many clients, you must be particularly selective, as this extreme behavior can negatively impact you and your staff through large amounts of time lost and scheduled time being disrupted. Below are some examples of "bad" clients:

- Clients who are excessively needy and compelled to talk about their situation endlessly to attorneys and/or staff members
- Clients who refuse to take responsibility for their actions and any contribution they may have made to the current breakdown, problem or dispute
- Clients who are deceptive in an attempt to protect themselves and their interests
- Clients who withhold information or stall in complying with your requests due to mistrust
- Clients who are so consumed with their dilemma that they cannot focus on or follow through with your instructions

Unless you practice "threshold law" (you take anybody who crosses your threshold), you likely have developed a means of identifying "good" clients. We have taken what you instinctively know about client selection and developed selection criteria to make the process easier and a little more scientific. This selection process centers on what we call the **client scorecard**—a form that enables you to rank clients in certain critical categories. By making the process quantifiable, you can now have members of your staff pre-interview and rate prospective clients on the phone. Especially if your initial consultations are free, this will eliminate your having to spend many unproductive hours interviewing what may turn out to be a "bad" client.

Case Study
Time Management Issue: Coaching Prospects Saves Time

Attorney: Harriett Steinberg
State: New York

After many years of practice, Harriett has developed great sensitivity to the timing issues inherent in the client selection process. When a marriage begins to deteriorate, a certain amount of time is required for both parties to work through the phases of shock, anger, and acceptance that accompany the process. Even for the initiating spouse, divorce is a lengthy process that shouldn't be undertaken prematurely. Harriett has gained the wisdom to recognize that if you sign clients up too early, you spin your wheels, spend their money needlessly, and don't satisfy them, because they weren't really ready to move forward. She now operates as a sort of coach with clients who come to her too early in the process. She encourages these clients to take stock and to consider other actions before hiring her and filing for divorce. Experience has shown it's a waste of her time to begin the process prematurely—even when the clients don't recognize this fact themselves.

Harriett's Good Advice:
Don't spin your wheels. Have the sensitivity to recognize where clients are in terms of readiness and give them recommendations that will support them. Having done this, you are guaranteed to see them return when they're ready.

Adopting the Client Scorecard Method of Selection

As you read through this discussion, look at the client scorecard that follows as Example 4-1. The categories on the scorecard are those we deem the most critical when it comes to selecting clients:

- Cooperation and credibility
- Ability to pay
- Case value
- Type of work (is it the type of work you prefer?)
- Referral source

Our ranking system is based on four levels: A, B, C and D clients. The A clients score the highest in each category; D clients score the lowest.

You can modify the form to suit your own needs. For example, some attorneys may assign a different weight to each category. Many of the attorneys we work with weigh the *ability to pay* pretty heavily. For these attorneys, a client who scores an A in every category but cannot pay for services is immediately downgraded to a D level.

For other attorneys, the *opposing counsel* category can be a deal-killer. Their experiences with some opposing counsel have been so negative that even if a client is a high scorer in every category but this one, they refuse to take the case. Alternatively, some of our clients simply raise the cost to the client based on what they fondly call the "jerk premium." They know that the extra work generated by the opposing attorney's tactics warrants the higher fee and openly discuss this with the potential client.

For an example of how a specific type of practice would customize a scorecard, here are the criteria used in a family law practice:

- Availability of assets
- Client personality and credibility
- Level of income
- Attitude toward children
- Case complexity
- Level of spousal animosity
- Opposing counsel
- Referral source

Read through our example of a client selection scorecard and use it as is, or modify it to suit your particular practice. Think about the clients you consider to be "A" level and those who have been "D" level. Add your own criteria to the scorecard to ensure that it reflects the issues you must consider before working with a client.

EXAMPLE 4-1: A, B, C, AND D CLIENT SELECTION SCORECARD

Rank	Client Personality	Type of Work	Case Value	Ability to Pay	Referral Source
A	Cooperative	Most Preferred Work	High Fees	No Problem	Very Good Work
B	Cooperative	Semi-preferred Work	Medium Fees	Slight Problem	Medium-Level Source
C	High Maintenance, Not Cooperative	Not Preferred Work	Low Fees	Low or Slow to Pay	Yellow Pages or Referred by C-Level Source
D	High Maintenance, Very Difficult	Work Outside Your Expertise	Low or No Fees	Very Low or No Ability to Pay	Yellow Pages or Referred by D-Level Source

Putting the Client Scorecard into Practice

> **"It is better to *not* do the work and not get paid rather than *do* the work and not get paid."**
> **—Jay Foonberg**

With this form you can now score potential clients and make a logical decision whether or not to take them. You can do this during or right after your first client interview, but you risk wasting time when there is a better way. We suggest that you create a system around this form that allows you to score the clients on the phone *prior* to their first visit and then, if they appear to be qualified, continue the scoring process when they come in. Remember, however, that it is not usually the best use of your time to screen potential clients on the phone. That is best left to staff who have been trained on how to use the client scorecard. The best situation is to have a designated **intake person** who is on the alert for desirable levels of clients and has a keen sense for financial and personality-based red flags.

What makes many clients "the wrong kind" is their habit of not paying for services rendered. Your accounts receivable report might indicate that you have not been the best at judging a client's ability to pay in the past. The questions that follow are very important, as the answers will suggest the degree of a potential client's financial stability. Any that indicate instability should be seen as "red flags."

- Did the client find you in the phone book?
- Was the client referred by a local bar referral service?
- Was the client referred by a C or D client?
- Is the client's first question "how much is this going to cost me?"
- Does the client mention that he/she knows another lawyer who is cheaper?
- Does the client resist paying a consultation fee or a retainer or only pay half?
- Does the client hold out the promise of other work in order to get a discount?
- Does the client mention that he/she is switching attorneys or has switched attorneys midstream?
- Is the client a distant family member with a large matter?

It is possible to have a plan to filter out prospective nonpaying clients. If any of your clients exhibit these warning signs, think twice about working with them.

Aside from financial risk, there might be personality-based warning signs that could indicate future problems. Pay attention to these signs before you admit these troublesome clients into your practice. Level C and D clients do not sneak into your practice unannounced. They usually arrive at your door waving several red flags and you let them in—usually because you need the money, and because you are hoping that the uneasy feeling you felt upon meeting them was just heartburn. Begin to trust that uneasy feeling. It might be trying to tell you that you are getting involved with the wrong kind of client.

- Did the new client show up with a full-blown crisis and demand your full and immediate attention right from the start?
- Did the client display a level of anger totally out of proportion to the matter?
- Is the client seeking revenge or does he/she have some other hidden agenda?
- Does the client want you to guarantee a particular outcome?
- Can the litigation client hear an objective, realistic appraisal of his/her case?
- Does the client have a bad attitude toward lawyers?
- Does the client act displeased no matter how well you take care of him or her?
- Does the client refuse to take responsibility for his or her own actions?
- Did the client arrive late to the first meeting and neglect to bring documents that you requested?

Case Study
Time Management Issue: Spotting Troublesome Clients

Attorney: Caroline Black
State: Florida

A prospective client came in for an initial consultation with attorney Caroline Black several years ago. She was a nice, well-dressed, professional-looking and attractive person. Caroline describes her as having an innocent "puppy dog" face. Caroline began working with her in good faith and discovered her client was extremely manipulative, always pulling strings, and distorting the truth to serve herself. Over the next three years, the client racked up $50,000 in unpaid attorney's fees and began forging her husband's name on checks. Willing to give her a chance, Caroline tried every reasonable means of working with her but finally had to cease representation due to the financial damage and emotional strain. Not surprisingly, this client went on to work with *six* more attorneys, all who no doubt believed her to be credible—at least at the beginning.

Caroline's Good Advice:
Get out as soon as possible when you discover that clients are manipulative, can't be trusted, and don't pay for your services. Don't continue to believe what clients say when it is not consistent with what they do. Have an **exit clause in your retainer** so that you are covered in case you need to pull out.

Atticus Tip:
When prospective clients mention that they have worked with one or more previous attorneys on the case they bring to you, it is a warning sign. Very often the other attorneys haven't been paid or were paid a small initial retainer to begin work. Always ask this question in the very beginning of your interactions with prospective clients: "Have you retained any other attorneys on this matter in the past?" If the answer is yes, proceed with caution. Before taking the client, call the other attorney(s) to learn the status of the case and listen for comments on your prospective client's behavior. This simple step might save you a great deal of trouble.

Suggested Scripts for Client Intake

When your staff person is conducting a client intake interview, he or she should ask questions that point to problem areas. It is helpful to have scripts for him or her to follow. The script provides consistency and thoroughness, and can serve as a training aid. Here are some ideas for scripts.

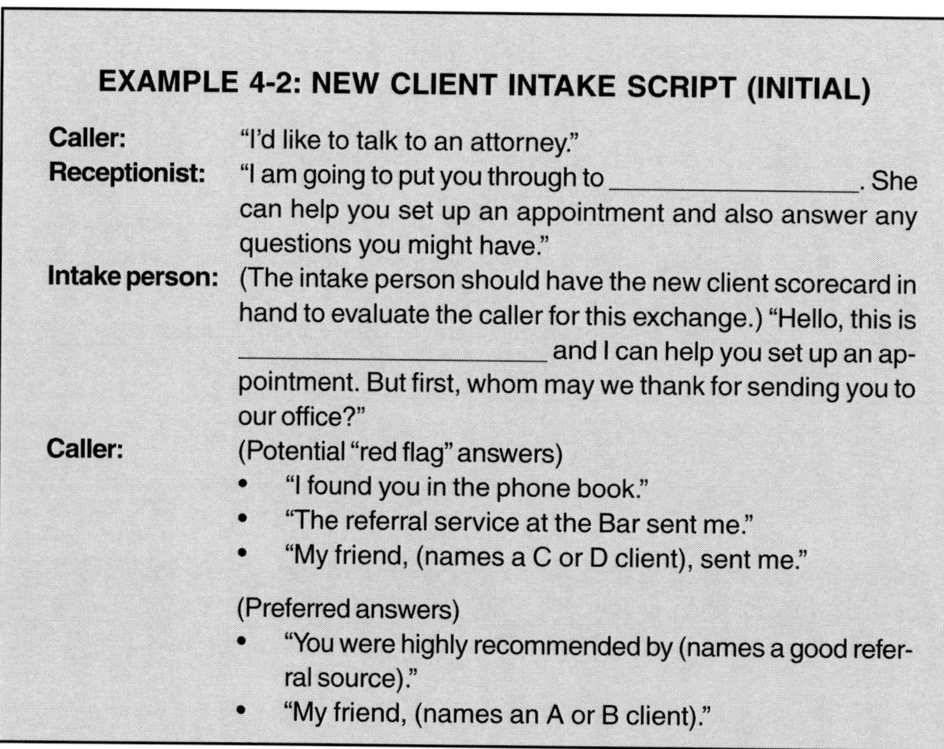

EXAMPLE 4-2: NEW CLIENT INTAKE SCRIPT (INITIAL)

Caller: "I'd like to talk to an attorney."

Receptionist: "I am going to put you through to ______________. She can help you set up an appointment and also answer any questions you might have."

Intake person: (The intake person should have the new client scorecard in hand to evaluate the caller for this exchange.) "Hello, this is ______________ and I can help you set up an appointment. But first, whom may we thank for sending you to our office?"

Caller: (Potential "red flag" answers)

- "I found you in the phone book."
- "The referral service at the Bar sent me."
- "My friend, (names a C or D client), sent me."

(Preferred answers)

- "You were highly recommended by (names a good referral source)."
- "My friend, (names an A or B client)."

The *red flag* answers tell you to proceed with caution. You may wish to move gracefully into mentioning the consultation fee, because clients who come from the red-flag sources named above will most likely be very price-sensitive, with the possible exception of the caller referred by your past client. When they hear the fee for the initial consultation, they may realize they've called the wrong law office, saving you from a client who won't pay. You may want to give them the names of some other attorneys who don't charge for their initial consultations. The tone of the conversation should always be friendly and helpful, not condescending, when turning away a client.

The *preferred answers* are the first indication that this may be a very good client and you should proceed with the conversation. Some lawyers prefer that the consultation fee be mentioned here. Alternatively, some mention fees after they go through a subsequent fact-finding conversation.

The next part of the pre-screening intake script requires a helpful, gently inquiring tone and shouldn't be rushed, as the intake person is inquiring about very personal issues. Not all attorneys are comfortable having their staff take it to the next level of questioning. This must be undertaken by someone with experience in dealing with clients, who is sensitive to their situation yet knows how to gracefully ask for enough information to qualify them. A long-time paralegal who has been acting as a "designated hitter" in your practice or an associate who has experience with clients qualifies. We discuss the term *designated hitter* in more detail in the next chapter of this book. For now, think of the designated hitter as someone who is trained to shoulder many of the lower-level communication tasks for the attorney.

The initial intake and the appointment pre-qualification are the first level of ranking using the scorecard. All the information gathered by the intake person is preliminary. However, it should be adequate to determine either that an appointment is warranted (because the client looks like an A or B client) or that referral to another attorney is more appropriate.

You will gather much more detail in the actual initial consultation with the client. It is helpful to go into the consultation armed with the facts, prepared for the client, advance information in hand, and ready to make a good impression. Clients who have been pre-screened have a much higher conversion rate than non-screened clients.

One of the most important skills for an attorney is the ability to attract clients. Without clients coming through the door on a regular basis, your law practice will not survive. Unfortunately, all clients are not created equal. The clients who appear with a page ripped out of the phone book are not quite the same as those sent to you by your best referral source.

How to Make the Transition to a Practice with Only Good Clients

If you find that you have stocked your practice with C- and D-level clients, it is time to conduct a housecleaning. Many attorneys are appalled to discover just how many problematic clients they have, but there is a solution. A lawyer who recently attended one of our seminars was so taken with the idea of finding out how many problematic clients he had that he went home and spent most of the night ranking his clients. As he suspected, the reason he was becoming so disillusioned with his practice was due to the fact that 80% of his caseload was made up of C- and D-level clients.

To conduct your own housecleaning, choose a time after hours when you are alone in the office or make it a group effort and go through the client list with your staff. Staff, by the way, usually have an unerring sense of who the A- and B-level clients are. They take the abuse that sometimes comes from C and D clients and know exactly who the more vocal or demanding ones are.

Take a Quick Look at Your Caseload

Before you begin, you can get some idea whether you have an overload of problematic clients by completing Exercise 4-1.

EXERCISE 4-1: SYMPTOMS OF A PRACTICE WITH MANY C- AND D-LEVEL CLIENTS

Instructions: Read through the following checklist. Place a check beside the situations that occur in your practice.

- ❑ High outstanding receivables—doing quite a bit of work for which you or your team will not be paid.
- ❑ Clients leave prematurely or often threaten to seek the services of another attorney.
- ❑ Clients fail to show for scheduled appointments.
- ❑ Clients fail to bring requested documents or to follow direction.
- ❑ Staff feel abused by clients who misdirect their anger and scream at them or act unreasonably.
- ❑ There is a constant sense of crisis and tension that is attributable to specific clients and/or specific opposing counsel.
- ❑ Staff and attorneys dread going to work and dealing with certain clients.
- ❑ Staff and attorneys are conscious of not meeting the high expectations of some clients.
- ❑ Staff and attorneys never hear "thank you" or any acknowledgment for their efforts—even when major victories occur.

Clean Up Your Caseload

If, according to Exercise 4-1, you have a practice with many C and D clients, you may be thinking about *how* to clean up your caseload. We encourage you to read through and take the steps listed here. You'll be surprised at how energizing it is to take control of your practice in this way.

- **Step One:** Go through your case list and rank your current clients A, B, C or D. Note the A and B clients, which you'll keep, and identify the C and D clients.
- **Step Two:** If you think any of your borderline C clients can be "rehabilitated" and upgraded to a B level, sit down and have a very straight conversation with them about what they are doing that is a problem (need to bring payments current, need to start producing documentation that is needed, need to stop canceling meetings, etc.). Some will respond positively to this approach; some will not. Take the rest of your C clients and refer them to another attorney if their issues are *personality-based*, not *payment-based*. Avoid sending clients who won't pay to another attorney.
- **Step Three:** Let your D clients go. Write them a letter, let them know in person, or phone them. Check your local rules to be sure you follow the proper protocol. If you decide to write a letter, your bar association likely has sample disengagement letters that you can adapt. In this chapter, we have also included sample forms and letters for your reference as Examples 4-3, 4-4, 4-5, 4-6, 4-7, and 4-8. If you decide to decline representation after research or investigation, you should protect yourself and your client by (1) promptly advising the client in writing of your decision not to take the case or matter; (2) informing the client of his or her right to contact another lawyer for a second opinion; and (3) informing the client that his or her prompt attention is required. Disengagement and non-engagement letters are especially critical when a lawyer decides not to continue past a specific stage in a case.

If you decide to let the client go in a face-to-face exchange, you need to have a plan. Refer to the guidelines in Exercise 4-2, How to Fire Clients Face to Face, to help you prepare.

EXERCISE 4-2: HOW TO FIRE CLIENTS FACE TO FACE

Instructions: Follow your local rules regarding releasing a client, especially if you are currently in litigation. (Your local rules supersede any advice given here.) Consider having a paralegal or legal assistant in the meeting if you really feel the client may react irrationally and later accuse you of misconduct. Under normal circumstances you won't have to take this extra precaution, but don't fail to document this meeting by summarizing the discussion in a letter and sending a copy to the client. Put a copy in your own file to protect yourself in case of a complaint.

Follow these steps:

1. Try to set the client up for the firing conversation and limit his or her reaction by saying, "You may not like what I am going to tell you, but. . . ."

2. Give the client the context for your decision so they will not think it is completely arbitrary. Link your decision to their attitudes and/or behaviors. Give specific examples of where the communication broke down, where they were uncooperative, where they were rude or abusive to you or your staff, or where they failed to pay.

3. Explain why the behaviors and/or attitudes expressed by the client make it uncomfortable, unethical or inappropriate for you to continue representation. Be factual and objective.

4. Give the client an opportunity to respond, ask questions or express anger. Resist being pulled into a discussion that escalates into a fight. Defensiveness only intensifies emotions. Stay in control of the conversation by managing your own emotions.

5. If appropriate, act as a helpful resource and make recommendations as to how the client should proceed. You may recommend counseling or a legal service agency, or offer the names of other attorneys who may help. (Remember to be very careful when referring unstable personalities and non-paying clients to your colleagues.) Call and discuss the situation beforehand to be certain the attorney wants to take this person on.

EXAMPLE 4-3: SAMPLE NON-ENGAGEMENT LETTER

DATE

NAME
ADDRESS
CITY, STATE & ZIP

RE: [SUBJECT]

Dear:

You have contacted this firm and requested that I evaluate whether the firm will represent you in the above-referenced matter. I met with you on [*date*], and have also reviewed the various copies of documents you left with me. I herewith return those documents for your use.

I appreciate the confidence you have expressed in our firm, but for various reasons the firm has decided not to represent you in this matter. However, if you have a need in the future for legal assistance, I hope you will again consider our firm.

You should be aware that the passage of time might bar you from pursuing whatever, if any, claim you have in this matter. Accordingly, because time is always important and could be critically short in your case, I recommend you immediately contact another firm for assistance.

In declining to undertake this matter, the firm is not expressing an opinion on whether you might prevail if the action is pursued. You should not refrain from seeking legal assistance from another firm because of any interpretation you may place on this firm's decision not to go forward with this matter.

In accordance with our standard policy, we are not charging you for any legal fees or expenses. While we do charge for evaluating cases, that is only when we express an opinion on the merits of the matter to the client. Since we are not expressing an opinion in this instance, no charge is being made.

Although I believe this letter fully covers all pertinent matters, please call me if you have any questions.

Sincerely,

[*signature*]

Reference: LOMAS, The Florida Bar, *Administrative Forms Handbook.* Reprinted with permission.

EXAMPLE 4-4: SAMPLE NON-ENGAGEMENT LETTER

(*May be sent by certified mail, with a return receipt requested*)

DATE

NAME
ADDRESS
CITY, STATE & ZIP

RE: [SUBJECT]

Dear:

The purpose of this letter is to confirm, based on our conversation of [*date*], that [*insert firm name*] has decided not to represent you because [*insert reason for declination; if possible and appropriate, state it*]. Our decision to decline this case should not be construed as a statement of the merits of your case.

You should be aware that any action in this matter must be filed within the applicable statute of limitations. I strongly recommend that you consult with another lawyer concerning your rights in this matter.

Very truly yours,

[*signature*]

Reference: LOMAS, The Florida Bar, *Administrative Forms Handbook*. Reprinted with permission.

EXAMPLE 4-5: SAMPLE NON-ENGAGEMENT LETTER AFTER REVIEW

DATE

NAME
ADDRESS
CITY, STATE & ZIP

RE: [SUBJECT]

Dear:

You have contacted this firm and requested that I evaluate whether the firm will represent you in a claim you believe should be filed against [*insert appropriate name(s)*]. I met with you yesterday and have reviewed various documents you left with me. I enclose those documents for your file.

I appreciate the confidence you have expressed in our firm, but for various reasons the firm has decided not to represent you in this matter. However, if you have a need in the future for legal assistance, I hope you will again consider our firm.

You should be aware that the passage of time may bar you from pursuing whatever, if any, claim you may have against [*insert appropriate name(s)*]. Because time is always important and could be critically short in your case, I recommend you immediately contact another firm for assistance.

In declining to undertake this matter, the firm is not expressing an opinion on whether you will prevail if a complaint is filed. You should not refrain from seeking legal assistance from another firm because of any interpretation you may place on this firm's decision not to go forward with this matter.

In accordance with our standard policy, we are not charging you for any legal fees or expenses. While we do charge for evaluating cases, that is only when we express an opinion on the merits of the case to the client. Since we are not expressing an opinion in this instance, no charge is being made.

Although I believe this letter fully covers all pertinent matters, please call me if you have any questions.

Very truly yours,

[*signature*]

Reference: LOMAS, The Florida Bar, *Administrative Forms Handbook.* Reprinted with permission.

EXAMPLE 4-6: SAMPLE NON-ENGAGEMENT LETTER—DECLINING CASE AFTER RESEARCH OR INVESTIGATION

DATE

NAME
ADDRESS
CITY, STATE & ZIP

RE: [SUBJECT]

Dear:

Pursuant to my letter of [*date*], we have conducted [*legal research or investigation*] to determine whether or not we felt you had a claim that could be asserted against [*insert appropriate name(s)*].

The result of our [*research/investigation*] indicates that there is not an enforceable legal basis for maintaining an action against [*insert appropriate name(s)*].

(*optional paragraph*)

Our opinion is based upon our preliminary research; however, we have found [*insert number*] cases that support our conclusion.

We urge you to consult another lawyer if you wish to obtain a second opinion. Time limitations may affect your rights to pursue a claim; therefore, you should act promptly in consulting another lawyer or otherwise pursuing your claim.

At this time, however, we are unable to proceed on your behalf. We are returning your original documents to you.

Thank you for your interest in our firm.

Very truly yours,

[*signature*]

Enclosures

Reference: LOMAS, The Florida Bar, *Administrative Forms Handbook.* Reprinted with permission.

EXAMPLE 4-7: DISENGAGEMENT LETTER—UNPAID FEES

DATE

NAME
ADDRESS
CITY, STATE & ZIP

Dear:

During the past [*time*], it has been our pleasure to serve you as counsel in [*subject matter title*]. In the course of that representation, you have paid us [*dollar amount already paid*] in legal fees and expenses. Unfortunately, contrary to our Engagement Agreement, you have not paid our statements in a timely manner for the past few months.

At this time, the outstanding and overdue fees and expenses total approximately [*dollar amount currently owing*]. Our firm desires to continue our relationship, but does not have the ability to finance your case. Moreover, you expressly agreed that the hourly fees and expenses in this matter would be kept current.

We have continued to represent you for the past [*time*], even though each month the outstanding fees and expenses increased. We did so because we value our relationship with you and would like to continue representing you.

At this point, in our opinion, the trial court will permit us to withdraw. There is still sufficient time for you to retain other counsel without jeopardizing your case or adversely affecting the court's calendar. However, if we wait several more months, it is possible that one of these conditions for withdrawal may not exist.

Your new counsel may wish to discuss this case with us. That would be to your advantage both substantively and economically. We are willing to do so as long as satisfactory arrangements are made to compensate us for the additional time and expense which will be incurred. In addition, it will be necessary to agree on a plan to gradually reduce the outstanding fees and expenses. We also have certain work product which has been generated during the past [*time*]. We are willing to share it with your new counsel to the extent our legal obligations require us to do so in the absence of full payment of our fees and expenses.

I enclose a petition for withdrawal which will be filed with the court ten days from your receipt of this letter. In the meantime, if you wish us to continue representing you, we would be pleased to do so if satisfactory arrangements are made to take care of the outstanding and overdue fees and expenses, as well as to take care of the future fees and expenses. I look forward to hearing from you, and remain hopeful the representation can continue.

Very truly yours,

[*signature*]

Reference: LOMAS, The Florida Bar, *Administrative Forms Handbook.* Reprinted with permission.

EXAMPLE 4-8: INITIAL CLIENT CONSULTATION INTERVIEW FORM

The purpose of an initial consultation is for the attorney to advise you, the *prospective* client what, if anything, may be done for you, and what the minimum fee therefore will be. *The purpose is not to render a definitive legal opinion* as it may be impossible to fully assess a matter within the time frame allotted for a consultation or with the (information or documents) that you may be able to provide at the initial consultation.

One of three outcomes is possible following your consultation.

A. **You and the Attorney mutually agree to the terms of representation, or** (After a separate document called an Agreement for Representation is signed, a copy will be provided to you.)

B. **The Attorney declines representation, or**

C. **You decide not to use the services of the Attorney.**

Note: The following questions will help us to understand the reason for your visit today. Your responses are protected by attorney/client privilege and will be held in strict confidence.

Name____

Last First Middle or Maiden

Address____

Number Street City State Zip

Home Phone (_____)________________

Briefly explain what you may need advice about or assistance with today:

____

____

____

Are there other parties involved? (Examples: a friend, an employer, a neighbor, signor of a contract, etc. This should include people or parties on either side of your issue)

Party______________________ Relationship______________

Party______________________ Relationship______________

Party______________________ Relationship______________

On the lines below, list the documents (papers) that you think may help us to understand the issues.

(1)________________________________

(2)________________________________

(3)________________________________

(NOTE: *Any documents you supply that are important to your matter will be photocopied, with your permission, and your originals returned to you at the conclusion of the initial interview.*)

Ideally, if things turn out precisely the way you want, what would the outcome be?

____

____

Knowing that there are no guarantees, what can you accept?

____

____

Please classify your urgency in concluding this matter. (Check One)

[ ] Critical—Personal safety or continuation of business depends on it.

[ ] Very important—Severe hardship, personal or financial inconvenience if matter is not resolved quickly.

[ ] Important—Matter interferes with business or personal financial stability.

[ ] Needs to be done, but no immediate hardship in the interim.

[ ] Just thought I'd see if it was worth pursuing, but I'm not counting on anything.

[ ] Just wanted to know what my rights are. I'll then let you know after I think about it.

If the matter involves payment to you of money you feel you are owed, how long can you wait before not getting paid?

____

(Days, Weeks, Months, Years)

Are we the first attorneys you have consulted regarding this matter?
[ ] Yes [ ] No

If No—Why didn't you hire their services? ________________

____

Have you ever been represented by an attorney before? [ ] Yes [ ] No

If Yes—Please state the circumstances ________________

____

How will you pay for your attorney's fees in this matter?

[ ] Check today [ ] Cash today [ ] Contingency Fee [ ] On Account

[ ] Credit Card ______________________________ ______________
Credit Card No. Expr. Date

Marital Status: [ ] Married [ ] Single [ ] Divorced [ ] Widowed [ ] Separated

Driver's License # ________________________

Social Security # ____ ___ _____

Are you known by any other names? [ ] Yes [ ] No

If yes what name(s)____
(A fictitious name, a nickname, a former name, your maiden name, etc.)

Where are you employed? ____________________________________

May we contact you there? [ ] Yes [ ] No

Phone No. (_____)_______________

If your mail is returned as undeliverable or your telephone service terminated, please provide the name of someone (friend or relative) you believe will always know how to contact you.

Name____

Relationship ____

Address____
Number Street City State Zip

Phone No. (_____)_______________

How did you learn of our office? [ ] A friend [ ] Yellow Pages [ ] Bar Referral [ ] Our Web Page [ ] Former client [ ] Other

PLEASE READ CAREFULLY & Sign Below

Following your initial interview, if you agree to hire the Attorney, and the Attorney agrees to represent you, you will both sign an Agreement for Representation. The Agreement for Representation will set forth the terms and conditions of representation.

If the Attorney is willing to represent you and you decide not to sign an Agreement of Representation today, you are strongly urged to schedule a second appointment with the Attorney at the earliest possible time or to immediately consult with other legal counsel to protect your rights.

***NOTICE:* This office does not represent you with regard to the matters set forth by you herein in this information sheet or discussed during your consultation, unless and until, both you and the Attorney execute a written Agreement for Representation.**

If the Attorney does not agree to represent you, this includes not representing you with regard to the matter set forth by you on this information sheet, or any other matters you may discuss with the Attorney during your consultation. If your legal problem(s) involve a potential lawsuit, it is important that you realize a lawsuit must be filed within a certain period of time called a Statute of Limitations. Therefore, the Attorney strongly urges you to ***immediately*** consult with another attorney to protect your rights. The Attorney's decision not to represent you should not be taken by you as an expression regarding the merits of your case.

Your signature acknowledges only that you received a copy of this completed information sheet and does not mean you have hired the Attorney.

SIGNATURE ______________________________ Date ___/___/___

****

This portion to be completed by the Attorney

[ ] Will represent (see New Case Memo and Agreement for Representation attached)
[ ] Will investigate and report (Schedule a follow-up conference for ____days)
[ ] Representation declined - Letter of declination will be sent.
[ ] Party will "think about it" and get back with us - No action to be taken and party was so informed.
[ ] Client declined Representation at this time.

Interviewed by ____________________ this ___ day of ________, ______

Notes:____

____

____

____

____

____

____

____

Reference: LOMAS, The Florida Bar, *Administrative Forms Handbook.* Reprinted with permission.

The Quality of Your Practice Is Equal to the Quality of Your Clients

As you can see, the quality of your practice is determined largely by the quality of your clients. Imagine how different your practice would be if you worked with nothing but A- and B-level clients. You might actually look forward to going into the office in the morning! They pay their bills, appreciate the value of the work you do for them, cooperate with you, show up on time, and send quality referrals. These are clients that you can actually enjoy. They are not completely crisis-driven and they trust your opinion. These are the clients who can get lost in the shuffle when you must scramble to handle the constant demands of your C and D clients. Every negative characteristic you can attach to clients means more time you will have to spend persuading them to trust you, calming them down, or trying to get paid.

Carefully selecting the clients you work with not only helps protect you against malpractice accusations, it also has the added benefit of saving you precious time, improving office morale, minimizing collection problems, and restoring peace in an otherwise crisis-driven practice. To better manage yourself, your time, and your practice, develop your client selection skills. The impact will be significant.

Chapter 5

Proactive Strategy Five: Schedule Like Tasks Together

Common sense tells us that setting a schedule is critical to successful proactive time management. In this chapter, we discuss managing your time by using your calendar and grouping similar tasks. This includes the introduction to an extremely helpful time management tool, the **time template**, some tips on how to use it, and how to introduce it to your staff to enlist support.

Time and motion studies reveal that performing similar tasks in the same time period results in increased efficiency. When you apply this theory to your scheduling habits, you'll dramatically improve how you manage your time. Lawyers find it especially helpful because when there are varied levels of complexity, performing like tasks together boosts efficiency. When your brain is allowed to focus on similar tasks, you can accomplish results four times faster than when you are continually switching the types of tasks or are constantly interrupted.

Contrary to what is most efficient, many attorneys are relentless multitaskers. That is, they attempt many different types of tasks at once and find that much stopping and starting ensues. It is not unusual to find the typical attorney with several layers of open files on his or her desk, talking to a client on the phone, signaling to the staff member in the doorway, and late for an appointment with a client.

This kind of work style promotes a feeling of anxiety, as the attorney wonders at the end of the day, or in a sleepless moment at 4:00 a.m., what important details were lost in all the chaos. The risk of liability goes up as chaos reigns. And rightfully so, given that many of the grievances filed against attorneys involve missed deadlines and/or disorganization.

Block and Tackle Your Office Tasks

To avoid this type of stress, let's look at how you might get started grouping like tasks in your office. We call this approach the **block and tackle** method. That is, once you "block" like tasks together, they are easier to tackle. You might think that the grouping process would be impossible, given the many different types of tasks you undertake, but we believe the nine categories of tasks we list below cover those that occur in the typical attorney's day.

1. Planning time (either once a week or daily)
2. Production time—Producing documents, supervising technical/legal tasks, preparing for trial, where applicable
3. Court time (where applicable, may alternate days with production)
4. Meetings with staff members, partners (general staff meetings, daily pre-production meetings, case status review meetings, partner meetings, etc.)
5. Meetings with clients
6. Time to return phone calls
7. Administration time
8. Time for client development
9. Time to systemtize your practice

The multi-tasker tries to do these tasks at the same time. This involves accessing different parts of the brain and never allows for great efficiency in any one task due to the choppy start, stop, and restart rhythm that is inherent in multi-tasking. For example, the reactive time manager reaches for the ringing phone no matter what he or she is doing. In addition to losing time, the quality of all the tasks suffers when dissimilar tasks are done concurrently. If you are in the habit of multi-tasking, you may be surprised at how much time the block-and-tackle approach saves you and how it increases the quality of your work.

Use a Time Template to Help You Block and Tackle

To put the time-blocking approach into effect, we suggest using a **time template**. A time template is a structure that enables you to separate all the types of tasks that normally occur in a typical week and block time for them to be done. For example, when there is complex legal work to be done, do only that; when it is time to meet with clients, focus solely on them. By working on one thing at a time according to your time template, you are increasing your overall effectiveness, and you have a visual reminder of all the critical areas of business on which you need to focus.

Here are two examples of completed time templates to give you an idea of what you will be working toward when you design your own time template. We have provided examples for attorneys who have regularly scheduled court appearances and those who have few court appearances.

EXAMPLE 5-1: REGULARLY SCHEDULED COURT APPEARANCE TIME TEMPLATE

The time template shown below is intended for use by the attorney who spends a lot of time in court. It features two mid-week client development lunches with time blocked for a Friday afternoon client development event (usually golfing, but other activities can be scheduled here). The case status review meeting as shown in this example takes place at lunchtime on Thursdays. Use this sample as a guide to creating a time template that works for you.

	MONDAY	TUESDAY	WEDNESDAY	THURSDAY	FRIDAY
9:00 a.m.	Plan Week	Court or Production Time	Court or Production Time	Court or Production Time	Court or Production Time
10:00 a.m.	General Staff Meeting				
11:00 a.m.	Return Calls	Return Calls Meet w/Staff	Return Calls Meet w/Staff	Return Calls Meet w/Staff	Return Calls Meet w/Staff
12:00 p.m.	Systemizing Lunch	Client Dev. Lunch	Client Dev. Lunch	Case Status Review Lunch	Client Dev. Event
1:00 p.m.	See Clients	See Clients	See Clients	See Clients	
2:00 p.m.					
3:00 p.m.					
4:00 p.m.	Production	Production	Production	Administration	
5:00 p.m.					

EXAMPLE 5-2: LOW OR NO COURT APPEARANCE TIME TEMPLATE

The time template shown below is intended for use by the attorney who does not spend a lot of time in court. This template features three client development lunches per week instead of two, eliminating the Friday afternoon client development event. The template includes a three-hour case status meeting on Friday morning.

	MONDAY	TUESDAY	WEDNESDAY	THURSDAY	FRIDAY
9:00 a.m.	Plan Week	Meet w/Staff	Meet w/Staff	Meet w/Staff	Case Status Review
10:00 a.m.	General Staff Meeting	Production	Production	Production	
11:00 a.m.	Return Calls	Return Calls	Return Calls	Return Calls	
12:00 p.m.	Systemizing Lunch	Client Dev. Lunch	Client Dev. Lunch	Client Dev. Lunch	Free Lunch
1:00 p.m.	See Clients	See Clients	See Clients	See Clients	See Clients
2:00 p.m.					
3:00 p.m.					
4:00 p.m.	Return Calls	Return Calls	Return Calls	Return Calls	Return Calls
5:00 p.m.	Production	Production	Production	Production	Administration

Schedule and Implement Key Time Template Blocks

Now that you have some background on the purpose and usefulness of the time template and have seen our examples, you may want to design your own. Before you take that step, you will benefit from some guidance on how to choose the right time to schedule certain tasks, how to determine the amount of time you need, and how to get the staff on board with the idea of working with a time template. We address each of the key time template blocks to help you focus on how you want your template to look and perform. We have combined comments about court and production time, because for some of you they may occur at the same time but on alternate days.

Key Block One: Plan Your Week

Weekly planning is the process of taking time to map out your week so that you are proactively making time for the achievement of both your long-term and short-term goals. Research tells us that one hour spent planning will increase your efficiency by a minimum of four hours. Remember this when you are tempted to just jump into your day or week; planning ahead of time doesn't set you back, it makes you more efficient. It may feel like you are wasting your time, but don't be misled by your own desire to jump in. Planning where to jump in and what to focus on is very important.

> **"It is not the strongest of the species that survive, nor the most intelligent, but the one most responsive to change."**
> ***—Charles Darwin***

Before you design your own time template, follow these ground rules to make sure you're on solid ground right from the start.

- **Choose the right time**. Find a time for your planning session that will not be bumped by court appearances or encroached upon by any other activity. Over what time slot during your week do you have the greatest amount of control? For most attorneys, Monday mornings or Friday afternoons are the best opportunities for a planning session.
- **Choose the right setting**. If your office is a place of stress and not a setting for reflection, find a more enjoyable spot where you can focus without distraction. Popular choices among our attorney clients are:
    - Home office, patio or deck
    - Coffee shop or breakfast place
    - The firm's library
    - The firm's conference room
- **Review the big picture**. To start your planning session, review your personal vision statement and goal grid. They will remind you of the personal life goals you have set for yourself and the strategic goals you have set as stepping-stones. Why review? The answer is simple: You will forget. Client demands and everyday urgencies compete for your attention much more successfully than your life goals do.

It is also a good idea to designate a **planning folder** and include the following items:

- Personal vision statement
- Strategic goals
- Client list
- To-do list

Finally, have your calendar either physically or virtually on your laptop or hand-held device. This is critical to your planning process.

When you actually map your own time template, after having taken the preliminary steps above, begin as follows:

1. Open your calendar and review one month out, three weeks out, two weeks out, and finally one week out.
2. Note the client meetings, mediations, marketing opportunities, court appearances, and any other events or deadlines on your calendar.
3. Work backwards from these events and deadlines by estimating how much preparation is required for each.
4. Look at your daily blocks of production time. Note the specific files you will address on your calendar. Make appointments with yourself to work on the "Smith" file or the "Jones" file so that you complete them prior to their deadlines.

Prioritize Before You Schedule

Before we move on to the other blocks on the time template, we would like to mention a critically important element in regard to creating your weekly plan: prioritization. Attorneys often find themselves overwhelmed by conflicting priorities. This sense of feeling overwhelmed is created by the barrage of new problems they face each day, and for many is triggered each morning when they look at their seemingly inexhaustible to-do list. You may be able to relate to this syndrome if you find yourself staring at your to-do list in the morning, choosing a task at random, and hoping that nothing falls through the cracks. This is a painful way to work, as most attorneys are goal-oriented individuals who strive to do everything all at once and do it well. The simple truth is this: Having too many priorities is the same as having no priorities. In the face of no clear priority, attorneys choose one seemingly urgent, important task that is easily done just to quickly check something off the list. Be aware, however, that urgency is quite often mistaken for importance.

It isn't always easy to tell the difference between urgent and important, and just because something is urgent does not automatically make it important.

Unfortunately, urgent tasks are generally much more compelling than those that are merely important. Think of the squeaky wheels among your clients. You often feel compelled to solve their problems at the expense of more cooperative clients just because they're making noise. When you stock your practice with high-maintenance, impossible-to-satisfy clients, you have introduced a lot of urgency in your life without much long-term gain. In such a practice, it is entirely possible to spend your days responding to the latest client crisis. That leaves important work undone, and at the end of the month you find that you spent a great deal of time on non-billable activities. Your profit margin will suffer if you attend only to urgent activities and put off important ones.

To keep yourself on top of what is truly important, we recommend that you **triage your to-do list**. To accomplish this, examine all the items on your list and rank them according to their importance. How can you distinguish what is most important among the myriad tasks on the list? You begin by looking for what we call the A (or highest) priority tasks.You can identify a task as A priority if one or more of these four questions receive a "yes" answer.

- **Does this task forward your long-term goals?** Long-terms goals are those that come from your overall vision, such as buying an office building, learning a new practice area, or cultivating new referral sources. Read your vision statements prior to planning your week to remind yourself of what is truly important.
- **Are there pending legal deadlines associated with these files?** Block out time for these tasks on your computer or delegate them to staff. These time-sensitive issues must be handled because they are extremely important.
- **Are there client expectations attached to this file or task?** Have you made a promise to a client to, for example, complete something by the end of the week? Always calendar these promises. These are your "soft" deadlines. They are not legal deadlines, but are nonetheless very important in terms of maintaining the confidence a client has in you. Monitor yourself to make sure you aren't consistently overpromising to the client and underdelivering. It is much better to underpromise and then overdeliver.
- **Are there cash flow needs that should dictate your next step?** You may interfere with your own cash flow by not focusing on production. Many attorneys are the bottleneck in their own system due to the number of files that accumulate in their office and remain untouched.

Once you have pulled out the A priority tasks, look for the remaining tasks on your to-do list—the B and C tasks. How do you tell the difference? Here are the guidelines for those tasks:

- B priority—tasks that do not require your unique talents or abilities and can be easily delegated.
- C priority—tasks that are not worth your time and attention and should absolutely be delegated or delayed as long as possible.

Take Priority-Based Action: Delegate, Eliminate, or Schedule

Now that you have triaged your to-do list, you have a method to plan intelligently. Delegate the B priority tasks and seek to eliminate as many of the nonessential C priority tasks as possible. Next, label the A priority tasks with a 1 (most important), 2, or 3, and take action accordingly. Let actions associated with your vision statement, legal deadlines, and client expectations drive your decisions. Though it may sound like work initially, once you are in the habit of triaging your tasks, your to-do list won't seem like one long, indistinguishable roster. It becomes more helpful because you have identified the truly important tasks. Use this approach to lift yourself out of the daily game of catch-up.

Key Block Two: The Three-Part Power Hour (Meet with Staff, Focus on Production, and Return Phone Calls)

The intention behind this block is to set yourself up to focus only on production for one to three hours at the same time every day. We have grouped three important blocks into one that we call the **three-part power hour.**

- The first time block is spent **meeting with staff.** It allows the staff to get their batched questions answered and could take from five minutes to an hour, depending on the workload to be discussed.
- The second part, the power hour itself, involves going behind closed doors and **focusing on production.** This block of time is for you to concentrate only on production and can last from one hour to several, depending on workload.
- The third part, **returning phone calls,** happens after production time.

Ideally, the power hour is scheduled in the morning before the challenges of the day set in. Fortunately, most people report that they are the freshest and most able to handle their complex work first thing in the morning. Unfortunately, many go to court with some frequency in the morning as well. We instruct attorneys who go to court quite often in the morning to block out their mornings as court/production time. That way, the attorney or the person who schedules for the attorney knows that if he or she is not scheduled for court, the time automatically defaults to production time, and the attorney will not be available for other appointments.

For those who cannot manage to schedule production time in the morning, the late afternoon is their next best time. Give staff members a copy of your time template for reference when scheduling your time in case you can't pre-block your calendar. Whenever it is scheduled, it is your private time of intense, concentrated production. Plan to spend this time wisely. Discipline yourself to focus on the most important, A-level, non-delegatable work you have.

An In-Depth Look at Meeting with Staff

Let's look at the first part of the three-part power hour formula: meeting with staff. The purpose of this meeting is to answer questions and to delegate items. A key strategy here is to instruct staff to group all their questions together and delegate tasks at this meeting. We call this technique **batching**. Batching refers to the theory that grouping questions together increases the efficiency of getting them answered with the fewest interruptions.

Many of the attorneys we work with meet staff members for 15 or 20 minutes in a quick "huddle" to talk about the goals for the day, give quick direction, answer batched questions, and delegate tasks. Some make this a half-hour or an hour-long meeting because they are supervising many files that have quick turnaround times. Use your own judgment on how much time this meeting must take. In this way, you train the staff to batch their questions and ask them in this meeting, thereby preempting many interruptions. The preempting of interruptions is one of the main benefits of scheduled staff meetings to answer batched questions.

You can also batch the questions and instructions you have for your staff, which forces you to be more organized when you delegate. We talk more about this in chapter 8, which focuses on delegation. This meeting is also an opportunity to ensure that all of your staff members have plenty to do while you are focused on your production. Remind your staff that they can get a lot of work done while you are behind closed doors. They usually appreciate the fact that you won't be interrupting them either.

An In-Depth Look at Focusing on Production

The second part of the three-part power hour formula is the time to focus on production. The purpose of this part of the power hour is to set yourself up for one to three hours of production without interruption, *behind closed doors*. We talk in depth in chapter 7 about more techniques and practices that will help you limit or eliminate interruptions during this time, but closing your office door is the most important one.

Since this way of working is a new discipline for you, expect that the first few times you try it will be uncomfortable. Once you get used to the power hour, you will come to view it as a sacred time during your day that is to be protected. Many of the clients we advise come to rely upon it as their island of sanity and as the space in which they can do their best work. Their production time gives them a sense of control over the chaos, especially when they've planned out their work in the beginning of the week. It is no longer a matter of using personal time to make up time that was stolen from them during the workday. For them, there is a newfound sense of control over their practice and a feeling that they can depend upon themselves.

In your production time, focus on tasks that can't be delegated:

- Producing documents, conducting high-level research
- Writing briefs, opinions, memos
- Reviewing discovery and deposition information
- Preparing for hearings, mediations and trials
- Reviewing work that has been delegated

An In-Depth Look at Returning Phone Calls

Let's look at the third part of the power hour—returning phone calls. The purpose of this block of time is to learn how to get work done and still maintain the appearance of accessibility. This is an hour during which you return the phone calls that have come in while you were "in production." Your assistant or call screener should have made call appointments for you while you were behind closed doors. We suggest instructing screeners to make the appointments at 15-minute intervals, if possible. Your return call schedule would look something like this:

11:00 – Mrs. Jones
11:15 – Mr. Johnson
11:30 – Mr. Roberts
11:45 – Mr. Smith

Or maybe only two calls came in and your hour looks like this:

11:00 – Mr. Lee (Said he needs at least 1/2 hour)
11:30 – Mrs. Jones

It is important that callers feel like you are still accessible to them, that their call is important, and that they are given a definite idea of when they will be able to talk to you. Always make your callbacks faithfully and answer whatever questions your clients have. Try to never sound rushed. If something comes up and you know you won't be able to call at the scheduled appointment time, have your assistant call and apologize and reschedule the call for another time.

One of the critical elements in this part of the power hour is to work with staff on screening calls properly while you are behind closed doors. The first rule, of course, is this: Callers should never be told to just call the attorney back. This is very unsatisfying to the caller. If he or she is a client, it seems uncaring, and it makes you, the attorney, seem inaccessible.

One way to work with staff on screening calls is to provide them with scripts that they can use or adapt to fit your particular situation. Here are a few phrases that your secretary, assistant or call screener can use to set up the appointments. The phrases in bold are important variations and communicate caring and a sense of rapport with the client:

1. "I know that Mrs. Attorney **would like to speak with you**. She will be returning calls at 11:00 a.m. Will you be available then? Great, give me the number where we can reach you. How much time do you think you'll need?"
2. "Mr. Attorney is not available right now **but I know he'll want to speak with you as soon as he can.** To make sure that you connect, may I set up a time when he can call you back? How does ____o'clock sound? Is that convenient for you? At what number may he reach you? How much time do you think you'll need?"
3. "Mr. Attorney is behind closed doors right now **but he'll be sorry he missed your call**. May he call you back between 11:00 and 12:00?"

In addition, when a phone call comes in, your receptionist should check to see if a designated hitter can help. A "designated hitter" is a person, preferably a paralegal, who, as mentioned before, shoulders much of the lower-level client communication burden of the attorney.

> "Mrs. Attorney is not available right now, but ____________ may be able to help you. Let me put her through."

If the designated hitter cannot help the caller:

> "Let me go ahead and set up a phone appointment so Mrs. Attorney does not miss you."

Key Block Three: See Clients

Another very important block in your time template is the time you reserve for seeing clients. In the reactive mode of scheduling, your time is up for grabs whenever you aren't in court. Clients can come in any time. In the proactive approach, your emphasis is on carving out time for production, then fitting other tasks around your production time. This includes seeing clients. For most of the attorneys we advise, the afternoon is the most popular time to see clients, as the attorneys are often in court or "in production" in the morning. They typically block off one to three hours a day depending on their caseload and typical new client intake rate per week. In addition, many report that their energy level is a little lower in the afternoon, and they prefer the stimulation of seeing and talking to people later in the day. This allows them to use their best energy for focused concentration in the mornings. If business is slow one week and they have an afternoon in which no client appointments are scheduled, they usually use it as extra production time to get caught up, to systemize their practice, or to conduct client development activities.

Case Study

Time Management Issue: Scheduling Time with New Clients

Attorney: Doug Sealy
Location: Nova Scotia, Canada

Doug Sealy provides his clients with a sense that they are being taken care of by always booking extra time for himself when he sees a new client. If he estimates the client meeting will take an hour and a half, he gives himself two hours. The extra time allows him to immediately draft an engagement letter. In it, he outlines the scope of work and the client's goals and objectives. He takes advantage of having all the details fresh in his mind. Then, even though he has many existing clients who are competing for his attention, he can quickly send the engagement letter out. This quick follow-up gives clients a signal right from the beginning that they are going to be taken care of. Every day that goes by after the initial meeting without the follow-up of an engagement letter erodes that feeling, no matter how successful the meeting.

Atticus Tip:
Some attorneys have their designated hitter sit in on their initial interview meetings with new clients. The designated hitter takes detailed notes while the client and attorney discuss their objectives and build rapport. These notes are the basis for the engagement letter. A checklist with a range of possible outcomes and objectives can be created to systemize this process, increase the accuracy of the notes, and save time.

At first it may seem too restrictive to offer a limited amount of time for client appointments. However, when offered several afternoon appointment times, clients usually will find a time that works for them without you having to offer any morning time slots. For the small group of clients who must come in the morning, we suggest you see them in the morning and swap your morning power hour time for time in the afternoon. This way you do not lose production for that day. Some attorneys occasionally see clients on a Saturday morning. It is acceptable to see clients on a Saturday morning, or even sometimes in the evening, if they rank as a good client with a lot of potential. You might even swap time out during the week or during the day if you know you are going to be seeing somebody on a Saturday or in the evening. Just try not to do this very often. The idea is not to have you working more hours using the time template, but to maximize your efficiency for the hours you do work.

As with your power hour block, it is especially important to block all interruptions when meeting with a client. Give the clients your complete attention in order to thoroughly interview them, understand their needs, and assess their goals. There is nothing worse than an attorney who meets with a client and takes telephone calls at the same time. You should never be interrupted with phone calls unless they are an absolute emergency. Allowing interruptions indicates to a client that you are insensitive or not that interested in his or her case. It is important to have clients like and trust you. Use your time with them to build rapport and determine if you can help them with their problem.

An important time-saving practice is to invite your designated hitter to sit in on this first conversation with a client so that you do not have to spend time getting someone up to speed if you are behind closed doors or otherwise unavailable. This person is key in making the time template work. We refer to designated hitters in several chapters of the book relating to their usefulness regarding interruptions and delegation. We have already mentioned the usefulness of the designated hitter as someone who is trained to take phone calls when the attorney is unavailable (see scripts for returning calls). The ideal candidate for this position is someone who is enough of a technician to handle the legal work delegated to him or her and enough of a "people person" to provide help to clients without disturbing the attorney.

Clients don't see this as a negative when a relationship with the designated hitter is established in the original meeting and they can call him or her to get their questions answered more quickly. Some law offices have the individual spend time with potential clients upon their arrival. He or she can preinterview them and get to know them before they go in to the attorney's office or conference room. This is especially useful if the individual is a warm and comforting person and the attorney is not.

Key Block Four: Case Status Review Meeting

Another very important block of time to dedicate in a new time template is something called the **case status review** meeting. This is a systematic way for attorneys to track and follow up on all the cases on which their staff is currently working. The attorney should leave this meeting with the feeling that he or she has been updated on the substantive and financial status of each case. These meetings, by the way, should not be confused with the short daily staff meetings that focus on short-term goals of that day. During a case status review meeting, individual files can be discussed and specific direction given in more detail.

If you are someone who does not delegate any work on your cases whatsoever, this is not a meeting that will interest you. However, most attorneys delegate to one or more staff members or associates. As confidants to many overwhelmed attorneys, we know that lack of a system to track and follow up delegated work is a common practice.

You may be someone who feels very out of touch with what is going on in your cases, which usually means feeling out of control and wondering every day what important detail, date or deadline you are missing. We have already talked about the high percentage of grievances against lawyers because of missed deadlines and disorganization. The potential for liability and client dissatisfaction is greatest in these situations: 1) when an attorney is trying to do all the work himself or herself and just doesn't have the ability; or 2) when an attorney is delegating work without a system to track it and ensure it is being done correctly.

Schedule Case Status Review Meetings

To begin holding a case status review meeting and tracking the financial status of each, you first block one or two hours a week or a couple of hours every other week on your time template. Choose a time that won't be commonly affected by the court system or other obligations and commit to attending this meeting without fail when it is scheduled. Emphasize the importance of the meeting to the staff (even if your staff is only one person) and have them regard it as an opportunity to get their questions answered.

Make sure that all relevant staff have the meeting scheduled on their calendars for the entire year. Once you start holding the meetings, don't tolerate absences or excuses. This meeting is too important to let slide. If you really desire a greater sense of control over your caseload, you must take responsibility for making the meeting happen. Don't hold it a few times, decide all is well, and then abandon the idea because you get too busy. This is a system designed to support you when you *are* very busy. If a truly legitimate reason arises that forces you to cancel the meeting, be sure that it is rescheduled, not just dropped. This meeting, when done right, allows you to supervise a greater number of cases by improving your efficiency, save time, and ensure that the needs and expectations of your clients are met or even exceeded.

Case Study
Time Management Issue: Crisis Interferes With Trial Preparation

Attorney: Divorce Attorney
State: New York

In a divorce practice, emergencies sometimes wreak havoc with the best-laid plans for the day. This client shared this not-uncommon scenario: Scheduled to start a trial on Tuesday, she had planned to go over all her final preparation on Monday. One of her clients had a crisis the preceding weekend and was able to resolve it only by agreeing that there would be a settlement conference on Monday. So she ended up doing the settlement instead of allowing herself the trial preparation that she wanted to do for the trial on Tuesday. She was up at the crack of dawn the next day working to make up for lost time. When the trial came, she had that sinking feeling of not being completely ready when walking into the courtroom. She vowed not to let this happen again.

Atticus Tip:
Whenever possible, try to block out time well in advance of your trial to give yourself a cushion in the event of a crisis. Never plan on having a crisis-free Monday. Too many crises begin over the weekend and end up as an emergency on Monday.

The frequency with which you need to review your caseload depends on how many cases you have that are open and active, as well as your tolerance for long meetings. In all cases, special time and attention are spent on the A- and B-level clients (refer to the client scorecard on page 24) to maximize the care they receive. Here are the two most popular approaches taken by our attorney clients:

- **The Once-Per-Week Review**—This schedule is for those attorneys who don't have a high tolerance for long meetings but have a large caseload to review. Divide the caseload, listed in alphabetical order, into quarters and review one quarter of the cases every week. At this level of frequency, it takes one month to review all the cases in your inventory.
- **The Twice-Per-Month Review**—For those attorneys who can tolerate a longer meeting, divide the caseload, listed in alphabetical order, in half and review half of the cases at each sitting. At this level of frequency, it takes two weeks to cycle through all of your caseload.

Whenever the meeting is held, all relevant staff members assemble in the attorney's office or conference room. They should have reviewed their batch of files in advance and preplanned their questions. The files are discussed one by one. In some cases the update only takes a minute or two, especially when there has not been any movement on the case. Other, more problematic or complex files will require a 5-, 10-, or 15-minute discussion. When problems are discussed, have the staff propose their suggestions on what should be done. Though the supervising attorney is always the legal authority, critical thinking should be encouraged among the staff where appropriate. Having the staff think of and suggest solutions educates them to be more proactive when working files. Often, afraid of making a mistake, staff members and even some associates are paralyzed by fear and unable to use their own judgment even within the limits of their job description. One of the solutions to this problem is the use of systemized checklists that we address in chapter 7. Basically, checklists help you keep track of what is happening with a file.

Many law offices spend an hour or two in the case status meeting and keep track of how much discussion time was spent per file in order to bill clients appropriately. Some don't keep track and don't bill for the time. If the discussion has been a substantive one, and the smallest increments of your billing program are not too large to apply, billing is appropriate.

Another way to approach this meeting is to meet with one staff member at a time to discuss just the files that are in that person's control. If you divide your practice among several disciplines and each staff member works with a different type of file, you may meet with each staff person and his or her files and have a sort of successive file review. Thus, you can either meet with individuals or all of your staff, depending on your practice mix. To make this meeting less tedious, you can hold it during the lunch hour and bring in pizza or other food while you are going through the cases. Your staff will actually look forward to the meeting if you make it a little bit fun.

Some attorneys we work with combine this meeting with their weekly planning time according to the time template. The attorney will do his or her planning in the morning, then a file review afterward, so they get an overview of all the files they are working on for that week.

Include Financial Status in Case Status Meetings

When the financial status of cases in your inventory are insufficiently tracked, it contributes further to a feeling of being out of control and may result in time and money lost. The case status review meeting is the perfect opportunity to start systemizing the tracking of the financial end of a case. If you have ever done a great deal of work on a case and not been paid, you are not alone. The experience of attorneys working diligently for their clients and not being paid appears to be universal. We have never worked with an attorney who hasn't been burned by nonpayment, often repeatedly. On some occasions, staff spent weeks or months working on cases where no fees were ever paid. This trend is so widespread that it has almost come to be accepted as the cost of doing business as an attorney. It doesn't have to be.

One of the reasons this problem exists is that attorneys have poor accounting systems. They may have great accounting software, but they don't look at their reports until it is too late. We have found that it pays to go beyond the cursory monthly review that many attorneys give their finances. You can incorporate a financial status review into your case status review meeting and create part of what we call the Zero-Tolerance Collections System. This method involves proper client selection, always receiving a retainer, and including a replenishment clause in your fee agreement. This combination of actions substantially reduces the amount of time you give away.

Case Study
Time Management Issue: Tracking Financial Status

Attorney: Divorce Attorney
State: New York

This client reminds us of the importance of tracking the financial status of all cases in order to maintain the profitability of a practice. She uses the term "not letting the work outstrip the money that is paid." A system should be in place to stringently keep the billing on a regular basis and to trigger a replenishment of the retainer if it falls below a certain amount.

> *The Attorneys Good Advice:*
> If the client does not replenish the retainer, see it as a tipoff that maybe the client is not able or not willing to pay.
>
> *Atticus Tip:*
> Regularly scheduled case status review meetings with financial reviews incorporated into them are efficient vehicles for keeping focused on the importance of profitability in a law practice.

Here are two easy ways you can incorporate the financial status component into your case status review meeting.

- **Bring your accounts receivable report to the meeting.** Before the case status review meeting have your bookkeeper print out an accounts receivable report by client. As the files are reviewed, check the report to review the financial status of the client. If there is a problem, you can, if appropriate, stop work on the file until the client's account is brought current. As the cases with outstanding balances are discussed, make a list of clients who need to be contacted and brought current. After the meeting, you and/or your staff make the calls to resolve the situation. (Note: The rules on stopping work while a case is in litigation vary from state to state. In some areas judges are sympathetic; in other areas they are not.) In any event, you should not find yourself preparing for trial or otherwise investing a lot of time in a case when you either haven't been paid or have no guarantee of being paid after the case is resolved. Take action early to prevent this from happening.
- **Invite your bookkeeper to the case status review meeting**. The bookkeeper (or whoever does the billing in your office) can systematically review the outstanding balance on a per-case basis. If the bookkeeper is at the meeting, a quick discussion can determine who should contact the client about outstanding payments, and the bookkeeper leaves with an action plan. Work is stopped or slowed when appropriate, and no one is putting time in that will never be paid. If a trial is approaching, a special "trial retainer" can be requested before work resumes (always check your local rules for compliance).

Three Side Benefits of Case Status Meetings

Once you start scheduling your case status review meetings, you will notice several side benefits of institutionalizing this kind of meeting in your monthly or weekly schedule.

- Staff know at all times the status of each case, making them more prepared to step in or field questions, where appropriate, without interrupting the lawyer.
- Increased ability on the part of the attorney to responsibly handle more cases. Because you are delegating a significant portion of the work, the number of cases you can handle rises, as does your profitability.
- The psychological benefit of holding this kind of meeting is the enhanced feeling of being in control of your caseload. You can forecast workloads more accurately.

As you work your way through the files in your caseload, you may notice that all have a different life cycle. This helps you in planning how much time is needed for certain types of cases. Some cases, such as a simple will in an estate-planning practice, are opened, worked on in a routine fashion, then completed. When all of the information is available, they follow a fairly predictable route. Other cases, such as a contested divorce with custody issues in a family law practice, are highly unpredictable and will make slower progress, with much stopping and starting. A complex case could be opened, worked on for several weeks, halted due to a change of heart, restarted and worked for several more months, then stopped, started again, and almost end up in trial—only to settle at the last moment. Some cases can drag on for years. It is important to identify the *unpredictable* cases and focus on working through the predictable ones as quickly and efficiently as you can to increase your control over your inventory.

Categorize Your Files to Predict Workload

Given that all files in your caseload are not progressing at the same speed, it can be difficult to assess how much work you actually have. How much of your time will they take up in your weekly and monthly calendar? Glancing at your case list will give you an overview that includes all matters currently open. It may not, however, tell you which files are on hold and require no action at this time. To help you get a true picture of the amount of work within your pipeline and how much time you need to allow, your files should be grouped into the following three categories:

- **Open-Active**—These are the files that are currently being worked. There are no obstacles to their completion and it is appropriate for work to proceed.
- **Open-Suspended**—This category of files include those in a holding pattern due to an impasse, lack of cooperation on the part of clients or

opposing counsel, nonpayment, or any other reason. These files should be discussed as to whether or not they will move from this category or stay on hold. It is useful to distinguish them from the "Open and Active" files, as there is no time being devoted to the files and they should therefore be set aside but tracked. The decision to complete or close the file will remain pending until something occurs to dictate its course.

- **Open-Need Closed**—These files are significantly complete and may lack one or two items before they can be officially closed. Unlike files that are open-suspended, finishing the file is dependent on actions that are within the law firm's control and not dependent on another source. Don't let a large number of these files linger on your case list, as they will just add to your sense of being overwhelmed. Better to finish up these files and move them into your longer-term storage system. If you have many of these cases, set a goal to close several a week until you get through them.

The next benefit to the case status review meeting is that it allows the staff to know what is going on with every file. That way, if a staff member who is not working the file takes a call regarding a specific file, he or she has some familiarity with what is going on in the case. Staff should be trained to elevate any substantive questions to you and less-substantive questions to the designated hitter.

Having the staff up to date on cases increases the likelihood that the attorney who infrequently delegates work to his or her staff will begin to practice delegation more often. Delegating to staff who are up to date can be a significant timesaving practice. This meeting also improves the efficiency of those attorneys who already delegate but have not systemized their practice until now.

Finally, there is no benefit like peace of mind. The psychological benefit of knowing that each case has undergone a systematic review impacts everyone in the office at all levels. You have set it up so that you and your staff are spending quality, prescheduled time on each case as opposed to spending catch-as-catch-can moments and dreading that something is slipping through the cracks.

Use a Case Status Review Form to Organize Meetings

To ensure efficiency and continuity in your tracking process, keep a succinct written record of the activity on each file. We have included Example 5-3, Sample Case Status Review Form, which accommodates the different file designations: Open-Active, Open-Suspended, and Open-Need Closed, as listed above. Use our form as-is only if you have a tiny caseload. Most law offices create their own spreadsheet so that they have a couple of pages dedicated just to the Open-Active file category.

EXAMPLE 5-3: SAMPLE CASE STATUS REVIEW FORM

File Name	Tasks	By Whom	Date Asgn.	Date Due
Open-Active				
Open-Suspended				
Open-Needs Closed				

By reviewing files on a regular basis and by combining this with the financial review and case-specific checklists for each file, you know each file is being touched on a regular basis and nothing is falling through the cracks. (Note that we cover creating and using case-specific checklists in chapter 6.) Hold these meetings as frequently as you need, and view them not as a tedious chore but as a tool that actually helps you manage and control the quality of a larger number of cases. We encourage you to create this worthy new practice for yourself and your firm.

Key Block Five: Meet with Staff

We view meeting with staff as absolutely critical to the success of a practice. With that commitment in mind, we focus on three types of formal meetings: case status review meetings, the meeting element of the three-part power hour, and general staff meetings. We have covered case status review meetings in depth because of their significance and detailed format. We provided you with some guidelines on the meeting element of the three-part power hour as well. In this next discussion, we give you some tips on general staff meetings.

In the general staff meeting, you inform the staff of your goals for the week and talk about upcoming court appearances. In turn, you discuss their goals for the week. Administrative issues may also be discussed, which might include systems implementation, timekeeping problems, or employee benefits issues. Some firms opt to have a short general staff meeting on Mondays and then go straight into their case status review meeting. If you are organized enough to do this on Monday, good work. It sets you up for a powerful week. If your practice typically is too fraught with crisis on Mondays because of events that have occurred with your clients over the weekend, a meeting later in the week works as well. If you hold your case status review meeting later in the week, you may be able use that meeting as double duty—case status review and general information exchange between you and staff. Keep in mind that the general staff meeting is less detailed—more an overview of the week—and may contain conversation about non-substantive issues. By contrast, the daily meeting is intended to contain the substantive issues you are dealing with that day.

However you decide to meet with staff, let them know that you will find a time after your planning session to bring them up to date on what your goals are for the week. This is true whether your staff is one person or a team of 10. Naturally, since your goals dictate many of their goals, it is important to meet with them and give them an overview of the time-sensitive issues on which you will be focusing. You may have the entire group participate in this meeting or you may decide it is more efficient to bring in one person at a time. It all depends on how much your team is cross-utilized.

Key Block Six: Attend to Administration

Partner-level attorneys have more work of an administrative nature than non-partner associates, but every attorney has administrative work to a certain degree. For partner-level attorneys, there is timekeeping and financial reports to review, accounts receivable and accounts payable to deal with, employee evaluations to prepare, and benefits package issues to consider. On your time template, this is a catch-all time block to capture all of the financial, staffing, equipment, and facilities-related tasks that come up on a weekly basis. Some weeks the demand for administrative time is greater than others. An hour may be fine for some, and for others grossly inadequate. If you are in a partnership where the administrative responsibilities are shouldered by several partners, the burden may be less. If you have a full- or part-time bookkeeper, the financial burden is definitely lessened. Given the makeup of your firm, use your best judgment to determine how much time you must reserve for yourself in this often overlooked but important block of time.

Key Block Seven: Systemize Your Practice

We believe that you, whether a solo practitioner or a partner in your firm, should block time every week to work on the systems that form the infrastructure of your practice. Typical projects should include learning new practice management software or developing a new intake system or a system for screening new clients. These are projects that do not get done unless someone is dedicated to making them happen, either by doing the job themselves or delegating it. We provide specific examples of systemizing in chapter 6.

A block of time, proactively scheduled, of one to three hours a week gives you the opportunity to either do the work or review the work that goes into systemizing your practice. It is an investment in the future that allows you to save many hours on repetitive tasks. This action puts you in the proactive camp and allows you to leave the reactive crisis mode behind. Your systems should be designed to save time and maximize profitability. It is critical to have staff participate in the creation of any new systems (i.e., new file opening protocol), as they are usually the ones to use them.

Monday and Friday seem to be popular days for these meetings. Some attorneys we know have lunch at their desks once a week and specifically dedicate that time to non-substantive projects. Some take themselves out to lunch and bring a project along to review at the table. Attorneys who are working on a project that involves members of their staff set a standing meeting for all relevant staff once a week if the need is great. Twice a month suffices if the office is fairly systemized already. A couple of attorneys work in their home office one morning a week on special systemizing projects. It provides a nice break in their week and allows them to work from home for short periods, which they really enjoy. Clearly, many systems projects need to be worked on in the office for maximum efficiency. Wherever you schedule yourself, find a time and a place where you will be comfortable and able to concentrate. Working on the business of your practice deserves your time and attention. Don't overlook it.

Key Block Eight: Develop Clients

Another very important block in your time template should be reserved for developing clients. When we first began advising attorneys on their practices, our main focus was client development. As we worked them through the process of developing new business, one of the most common complaints we heard was "I don't have time to market." As legal practice advisors, we suggest that you must proactively make the time to market. Your very practice depends upon it, unless you are so swamped with business that you never have to worry. If so, skip this discussion and dedicate your time to production and seeing new clients. Most attorneys, however, need to cultivate new business even when they are busy. Troughs sometimes follow peaks in demand.

We believe that the best, most loyal, and least price-sensitive clients come from referral sources who know, like, and trust you. Developing this level of rapport with referral sources does not happen overnight. It takes time for the relationship to build. Clients may come from a new referral source after just one or two meetings, but most likely it takes several contacts for the referrer to get to know you well enough to recommend you. The time and repetition that client development requires makes it something of a numbers game. We recommend three substantial marketing contacts a week. Three lunches are ideal. If you block out three lunches a week and dedicate them to marketing, that results in approximately 150 marketing lunches on a yearly basis. This provides a lot of time to maintain rapport with existing referral sources as well as cultivate new ones.

Whatever number of lunches you decide to dedicate to marketing, you need to block them out and stick to them. Seeing them blocked out on your calendar makes it more difficult for you to "forget" to market yourself. This is when the real value of the time template becomes apparent. It is a structure of support and a visual reminder for you to always think ahead about what clients or influencers you can take out to lunch to fill those slots.

It is helpful to have an assistant to work with you to keep your lunch schedule filled well in advance. Supply the assistant with a list of existing influencers you wish to see on a regular basis and the cards of new contacts you meet as you interact in the community. This can be a huge help, especially if you are bad about taking the time to initiate lunches.

An alternative to the marketing lunch idea is to have a standing Friday afternoon or Wednesday afternoon time block that is dedicated to marketing. For many of our clients who play golf, the Friday afternoon golf game is a popular marketing strategy. This strategy allows them to invite one to three other people to join them in golf on a weekly basis. That amounts to some 50 golf games over the course of a year. When multiplied by one to three people, the result is a minimum of 50 and a maximum of 150 marketing contacts yearly. Given the amount of time available when playing golf, there can be a significant amount of rapport-building with referral sources and important friends of your firm.

We instill our clients with the idea that there must be continual "top-of-mind" awareness regarding word-of-mouth marketing. People must remember you. The way they remember you is by having a variety of interactions with you throughout the year. These interactions can take the form of a telephone call, a lunch meeting, or an evening event. Many of our clients put a once- or twice-monthly evening event on their template to which they invite referral sources and their spouses out to dinner or to some other function, such as a community event, charity function, or gallery opening.

You can plan marketing events that also allow you to spend more time with your family, which is most likely one of your personal goals. You can invite referral sources and their families to outings and events such as a picnic or barbecue in the park, a pool party, a boating excursion, or a sporting event. Going to a game with your son or daughter and inviting referral sources to bring along their kids is a great way to also spend more time with your family.

Use your time template to structure your client development efforts. It is important to institutionalize your marketing time blocks, because you will find you never have the time to market unless you take this proactive approach and aggressively carve out time in your schedule.

Design Your Own Time Template

In Exercise 5-1, you are provided with some guidelines to help you compose the first draft of your time template. Refer to the examples you have seen earlier in this chapter and use the information given on the key blocks. As you continue to practice, you will soon be in control of your valuable time and not a victim of reactive time management.

EXERCISE 5-1: DESIGN YOUR OWN TIME TEMPLATE

Instructions: Look at the two time template Examples 5-1 and 5-2 provided earlier in this chapter: Regularly Scheduled Court Appearance Time Template and Low Court Appearance Time Template. Decide which one best fits your type of practice. Using the blank weekly time template provided, create time blocks for the nine key activities listed below.

1. Plan your week.
2. Production—Producing documents, preparing for trial, and supervising technical/legal tasks (may alternate days with court).
3. Court time (where applicable, may alternate days with production).
4. Meet with staff in various types of meetings (general staff meetings, daily pre-production meetings, case status review meetings).
5. See clients.
6. Return phone calls.
7. Attend to administration.
8. Develop clients.
9. Systemize your practice.

Weekly Time Template

Use this blank weekly time template to work out your own weekly time blocks. Remember to indicate the designated time blocks on your office calendar as well. Give each staff member a copy of this template so that he or she can keep it handy when screening your calls. Your staff can use these blanks to create their own time templates as well.

	MONDAY	TUESDAY	WEDNESDAY	THURSDAY	FRIDAY
9:00 a.m.					
9:30 a.m.					
10:00 a.m.					
10:30 a.m					
11:00 a.m.					
11:30 a.m.					
12:00 p.m.					
12:30 p.m.					
1:00 p.m.					
1:30 p.m					
2:00 p.m.					
2:30 p.m.					
3:00 p.m.					
3:30 p.m.					
4:00 p.m.					
4:30 p.m.					
5:00 p.m.					

Plan Your Weekly Appointments with a Planning Sheet

Now that you have your time template in place, you have control of blocks of time in your week. What you don't know at this point is what appointments you need to make, what administrative duties you have to attend to, etc. Make decisions regarding exactly what you will attempt in a given week with the framework of the time template in mind. To assist you in doing that, we have provided you with Exercise 5-2, a blank Weekly Time Template Block Planning Sheet. Make a master copy of the blank sheet and then follow the instructions. As you fulfill your commitment to your weekly planning hour and become skilled at planning week by week, you may no longer need this tool to help you through the process. In the beginning, however, it gives you added support in staying on target.

EXERCISE 5-2:
WEEKLY TIME TEMPLATE BLOCK PLANNING SHEET

Instructions: Review your personal and professional vision statements, then your calendar. Work backwards from upcoming deadlines and court dates to block preparation time in advance on your calendar.

PRIORITY PRODUCTION:
What are your most important production goals this week? (Set appointments for these tasks in the "Production Section" of your Weekly Time Template.)

______________________________ ______________________________

______________________________ ______________________________

PRODUCTION SUPERVISION:
List the most important tasks you are supervising/tracking this week.

______________________________ ______________________________

______________________________ ______________________________

MARKETING ACTIVITIES:

Who will you initiate contact with? Attend lunches with?

______________________________ ______________________________

______________________________ ______________________________

SYSTEMS/OPERATIONS:
How will you improve your systems/operations this week?

______________________________ ______________________________

______________________________ ______________________________

ADMINISTRATIVE GOALS:

______________________________ ______________________________

______________________________ ______________________________

STAFFING:
What can you do to—
- Acknowledge/reward/motivate staff? ______________________
- Train staff? ______________________
- Hire staff? ______________________
- Meet with your designated hitter? ______________________
- Practice delegating more? ______________________

PROFITABILITY/FINANCIAL GOALS:

______________________________ ______________________________

______________________________ ______________________________

FAMILY/PERSONAL GOALS:	**EXERCISE GOALS:**	**SPIRITUAL GOALS:**
____________________	____________________	____________________
____________________	____________________	____________________
____________________	____________________	____________________

Ensure Support for the Time Template Concept from Staff

It is important for your staff and the other attorneys in your office to understand why you are attempting to implement a time template. You really need the support of other people to make it work. We suggest sitting down with your staff and explaining to them the concept of the time template. You are the first line of defense when it comes to implementing and enforcing your time template and your self-management. However, if your staff members are not enrolled in the idea—if they do not recognize the value and the importance of the time template—they can be the first ones to sabotage it, even though they may have the best of intentions.

Because the time template concept is new and different, we have included a script to follow as Example 5-4, Conversation with Staff Regarding the Time Template. It is helpful to use our language, or at least be guided by our language, when enlisting support for your new time management plan.

EXAMPLE 5-4: CONVERSATION WITH STAFF REGARDING THE TIME TEMPLATE

We know that part of the difficulty in implementing a new habit like the use of a time template lies in explaining it to your staff and co-workers. You need their support to make your new way of calendaring successful. Many of our attorney clients have stumbled when trying to voice this new direction. We have put together some sample language for you using phrases that clearly identify the concept. Have your time template handy to illustrate your discussion. It is valuable to have one for each member of the team.

Open by Asking for Their Support
In this initial part of the script, ask your staff and co-workers for help in managing your time a new way. Given that they have all been used to scheduling your time or helping you organize your time in the past, it is important to let them know (1) what the time template is; and (2) why you want to change how you manage your time.

> "I need your support to help me manage my time better. As you know, I end up working a lot of weekends and evenings, trying to get all my work done, and I think that by organizing my calendar differently, and with your support, I can work more normal hours."

Explain That the Time Template Is Not a Calendar
Next, explain what the time template is, and what it is not. It is important to explain that the time template is a new approach to calendaring time, but it is not an actual calendar. It is a set of new calendaring rules that allow for certain activities at certain scheduled times.

> "I am going to work more normal hours by making better use of my time when I'm here in the office. I am going to manage my calendar in a new way, using something called the time template. The time template is not a calendar. Do not confuse it with a calendar. We will continue to use our existing calendaring system. It is more a set of rules for my calendar that will stay the same, week after week, and will allow me to create a template for my week."

Mention the Typical Time Template Time Blocks
Show the time template as you explain the following:

> "By following the time template, I will have time for everything that I need to do, but I will not be trying to do it all at once. There will be a standardized time when I plan my week, meet with all of you, work on my files, review all the files, do my administrative work and attend client development lunches."

Give More Detail on Your Production Time or Power Hour

Emphasize the importance of your production time:

> "For example, on my time template, I am going to block out the same time every day to concentrate on my highest-priority production. I will typically do this every morning—whenever I am not scheduled to be in court. So, any morning that I am not in court, I will use for my production time, and during my production time, I will be behind closed doors, working on the files and the cases that are my priorities. To avoid distractions, I am going to close my door during my production time, and because we are used to an open-door policy around here, this will take a little getting used to, but please do not interrupt me unless it is a real emergency."

Ask for Their Support in Minimizing Interruptions

> "I need for you to help me protect my time behind closed doors. We need to set up my calendar so that this time is blocked off, and no client appointments are scheduled or phone calls put through during this time. When somebody calls, you [direct this to the person or persons who are most likely to field your calls] will set up a phone appointment with them so that when I finish production, I can call them immediately. I'll have a 'return calls' block scheduled in my calendar that will allow me to return phone calls at that time. I will be behind closed doors between 9:00 and 11 :00 [insert your own times], and returning phone calls between 11:00 and 12:00 [insert your own times]."

Teach Them About Question Batching

> "I will also be incorporating a daily staff meeting so that before I go behind closed doors, you can get all of your questions answered. I will meet with you between 8:00 and 9:00 [insert your own times]. It is important that you learn to batch your questions and hold them for when we meet. 'Batching questions' means keeping track of all questions that arise that require you to stop working on a file because you have to ask me for direction. Don't run in and ask me the question. Instead, jot down your question, and we will address it in the next meeting. Continue working on the next file. If we are meeting before you have any questions, open the files you'll be working on in the coming day and try to anticipate questions. Write them down and we'll address them all at once."

Explain How the Time Template Helps Them

"Not only will these daily meetings help me because there will be fewer interruptions during my day, they will also help you. You'll be able to count on my availability to you between 8:00 and 9:00 [insert your own times]. You won't continually be trying to track me down to get your questions answered so that you can finish your work."

Explain the Other Time Blocks in the Time Template

"I am also going to reserve time for a weekly planning session, in which I will review the calendar and look at all of the hearings and trials that are scheduled, the client meetings, and other deadlines already set. I am going to reserve my afternoons to see clients, so whenever a new client calls, we will automatically schedule them into the first available afternoon. At the end of my day, I am going to block another hour of production with time to return phone calls immediately afterward. By blocking my time this way, I know I will have given myself enough time to accommodate the clients that want to see me, handle phone calls during the day, and complete my highest-priority production. If I do this right, I won't have to work in the evenings and give up my weekends any more."

Close with a Final Request for Their Cooperation

"I would really appreciate it if you would support and enforce this time template. I give you my permission to remind me when I get off track. Please post this time template near the phones to remind you of when I am and am not available so that you can hold my calls when I am behind closed doors and make my client appointments and phone appointments fit within the appropriate time blocks. I would appreciate it if you commit to following these new rules that I have set up. I think it will help us get a lot more work done around here, and help everyone to go home on time, so that nobody has to work on the weekends."

Chapter 6

Proactive Strategy Six: Systemize Your Office

Thomas Leonard, seen by many as the founder of business coaching, dubbed problem-free environments "crisis-free zones." Many of the proactive time management strategies we've already discussed will help you reduce the number of crises you encounter and allow you to maintain better control of your time. Despite your best efforts, however, you may still find yourself in an environment where one crisis after another is the norm.

A number of different factors contribute to an office crisis; some you can control, and some you cannot. Clients, even A and B clients, will have unexpected problems. And you can count on referral sources, partners, or your opposing counsel to have issues that will demand your immediate attention. The control you have over crises instigated by *external* influences is limited by your ability to choose your clients, referral sources, and partners wisely.

Aside from making good external choices, you must also do what you can to eliminate crises that arise *internally*. Issues such as poor office protocol, a lack of written office procedures, and piles of files increase the chance of something falling through the cracks and creating a problem.

To reduce internally created crises and adhere to your time template, you must **systemize** your office practices. In this chapter, we focus on creating systems for three areas that commonly create problems. The areas we target are:

1. Establishing a system of checklists that direct the sequence of activities in each type of file
2. Establishing model files for each type of case or matter that you typically handle
3. Establishing an efficient filing system on your desk to process paper

Checklists are written procedures that are created to demonstrate the best way to work through every type of file in your office. We explain the checklist system, tell you how to make checklists, and give you some guidelines for putting them into practice. We also give you a technique for institutionalizing a model file that can reduce lost time. Finally, we tell you how to establish an action-oriented filing system on your desk that can save you time currently spent searching for lost information. The paperless office is not a reality quite yet, and those "piles of files" on your credenza, floor, and desk are not going to disappear on their own.

Why Systemize?

Law offices tend to rely upon "customary" ways of doing things. This occurs most frequently in what we'll call the "personality-driven" law office. In these situations, attorneys rely on longstanding employees who have supported them for years. Perhaps staff were trained to work through a file a certain way, or perhaps they use procedures they learned at a former law firm. Very often the customary office procedure is simply what they have observed and gotten into the habit of doing year after year. Unfortunately, the "customary" ways are not usually written down.

"When a fixed procedure is too long to be memorized economically . . . checklists or some other queuing mechanism . . . enable the man to become familiar with the task during training and to perform independently in a field situation."

—Leslie J. Briggs, American Psychological Association

So what happens when new hires come in and try to work their way through a file? The training they receive is dependent on how those around them articulate the process. Training is especially difficult and somewhat unreliable when organized written references don't exist because your office is not systemized. Since the rate of staff turnover is always increasing, this is a critical issue not only for training, but for quality control as well.

Establish a Checklist System

As we have said, the checklist is a critical element of the systemized office. For every major type of file that you work on, there should be a checklist. The checklist is a step-by-step list of each activity or task that occurs within that file in the appropriate sequence, with a place to denote the due date and a place for staff to initial when the task is complete. The goal is this: Any person who picks up a file should be able to see exactly what has been done, because every task has been identified, put in sequence, checked off, and initialed upon completion. In short, everyone can rest assured that nothing has been missed.

Once the checklists have been thoroughly analyzed and found to be efficient, they should be termed **master checklists**. For ease of reference, for training new hires, or for retraining, these master checklists should be stored in two places:

- On your computer in the appropriate public directory
- In hardcopy, in a binder for each type of file (uncontested divorce, contested divorce, living trusts with tax planning, living trusts without tax planning, etc.)

Create Easy Access to Master Checklists

By putting the master checklist on your computer network, you make it accessible to everyone. You can create a folder labeled "Checklists," with sub-folders that are labeled according to type of file—for example, Contested Divorce. Encode each individual type of checklist to reflect the latest versions. If you have invested in case management software for your practice, you may be able to incorporate your checklist into the software if it doesn't already provide this function. Another benefit to storing them on the computer is that it serves as a backup for the hardcopy binder. You can divide the sections with tabs to allow for ease of use. Below is a suggested tab system for your hardcopy binder listing the tabs, their order, and the purpose of each:

1. **Master checklist:** Behind the first tab, include a copy of the master checklist (e.g., contested divorce, DUI).
2. **Procedural notes:** Behind the second tab, include procedural notes—anything that is too lengthy to explain in the checklist itself. This allows the reader to obtain a more lengthy explanation of certain steps listed in the checklist.
3. **Samples:** Behind the third tab, include samples of the documents referred to in your checklist. These will be documents commonly used in this type of case, such as sample pleadings, affidavits, orders, questionnaires, and letters.

The ability to train and retrain people on your particular procedures is critical to preempting crises. Having checklists like this serves as a reference tool for existing employees and as a training tool and ongoing reference tool for new employees.

Several Ways to Create a Master Checklist

We have talked about how the checklist system works and how to create a checklist. Let's go into detail on the topic of creating the actual master checklist for your files.

There are basically three approaches to creating a master checklist. When you, the attorney, analyze and list the tasks for specific types of cases or matter types and construct the checklist, we call it the "Analyze and Create the Checklist" method. In the second method, you select another individual in the office to participate in a process we call "I'm a File." The last method we call the "File in Action" approach, in which the checklist is created by the entire team.

The "Analyze and Create the Checklist" Approach

If you decide to create the master list, follow these steps:

1. Select a common type of file or matter.
2. Write the protocol (non-substantive activity) for opening the file based on how that type of file is typically opened.
3. Write the protocol (non-substantive activity) on how that type of file is typically closed.
4. Look at the most commonly repeated activities within the file and determine the steps (substantive activities) that take place as the matter or file is worked (e.g., prepare documents, acquire records, schedule depositions).
5. List the steps in outline form.
6. Provide a place beside each step to mark the due date and a place for the person who is working with the file to initial when complete.
7. Where it is appropriate, list references to relevant documents by name or by their location in the computer.

The "I'm a File" Approach

To create the master checklist by using the "I'm a File" approach, you, the attorney, write the protocol (non-substantive activity) for opening and closing the file based on how that file is typically opened and closed. However, you delegate the task of writing the actual checklist to save time.

Case Study

Time Management Issue: Systems Save Time and Energy

Throughout our years of working with attorneys and helping them get back in touch with their hobbies, passions and interests, a number of them decided to obtain their pilot's license. Almost without exception, they've acknowledged that they didn't fully appreciate the benefits of checklists and systems until they took flying lessons. Typically, what they came to realize is that the riskier the endeavor, or the higher the need for quality control and predictability, the more systems are created and relied upon. While the problems solved by lawyers are not always a matter of life and death for their clients, there are many cases that carry substantial risk for both the lawyer and client. Preempting problems and managing that risk is important to all attorneys.

To learn how checklists and systems preempt problems and help manage the everyday risk inherent in aviation, we interviewed G. Patrick Owen, a former carrier pilot instructor with the United States Navy, and current pilot and flight instructor for Northwest Airlines. We were curious to learn whether or not the systemization approach taken in aviation would offer insight into creating and adhering to systems in the law office. Below are the results of the interview.

Pilot: *George Patrick Owen*
State: *Florida*

What are the benefits of systems and checklists when flying an airplane?
There is one overriding goal when flying a plane: a safe, efficient operation that results in a successful landing at the intended destination with minimal distractions. Anything that impedes the means to do this must be viewed as a distraction. This goal applies despite weather, time of day, or the financial condition of the airlines. Landing at night on automatic pilot should be the same as landing during the day. The airplane doesn't "know" it's night. Systems cut down on mechanical and mental fatigue. That includes the automation of the mechanical systems of the airplane and the checklists for operating procedures. You get predictable results v. random results. Checklists save time because you're not re-inventing the wheel every time you face a task. Effective systems take the emotion out of decision-making.

Do some pilots resist using systems and checklists?
Those individuals who don't like checklists or systems don't make it as pilots. There's a reason commercial airlines have more than one pilot in every cockpit. They don't want anybody going off on a creative tear without checks and balances. They want a team to support the checklist and the systems.

What are the consequences of not using systems and checklists?
Without systems, you get inconsistent results. Checklists are designed to take care of the minutia and that leaves brainpower to focus on core issues. Minutia encompasses maintaining altitude, keeping wings level, and engine rpm tuning. The core issues to deal with are weather on arrival, fuel for holding if necessary, and the status of aircraft systems (i.e., brakes).

Are some systems more important than others?
The priority goes like this:

#1 Systems that aviate (keep the airplane in the air)
#2 Systems that navigate (keep the airplane going in the right direction)
#3 Systems that communicate (This is the least important. You don't talk until you have the airplane flying and know where you are going.)

How does one discipline himself or herself to adhere to the checklists?
Once you learn the systems, you begin to have faith in them. You find that you get a superior result with less effort. The systems allow you to critique yourself immediately after every flight. What went right? What went wrong? What could be improved?

What advice do you have for those who don't naturally have faith in checklists and systems?
See checklists as building blocks. You have to walk before you can run. Don't beat yourself up if you fail. Look for skilled peers to show you how to do better. There is no substitute for being prepared. All the important decisions need to be made in a controlled and calm environment on the ground. You don't have to deviate from the plan unless there is something of impending importance that requires it. It's rare.

If you make a serious mistake, you ask yourself, "Is this the beginning of the new beginning or the beginning of the end?" Attitude and openness to correcting mistakes determine the new direction. People become afraid if they don't have all the answers up front. You have to accept that you will never have all the answers at given points in time. If you are adequately prepared, you will get the answers, as you need them.

Many people can be brilliant pilots if they have great weather, plenty of gas, and an airplane in good condition. Only when something goes awry, do they then have to multi-task in high stress environments. Pilots, for the most part, are not paid for what they do; they are paid for what they know.

To begin, assign one staff person to walk through the office, stopping at every location that a particular type of matter, case, or file would travel as it is worked. By interviewing each person who works on the file, the staff person can come up with the steps that are most commonly taken and in what sequence in this type of case. The interview may take place with two people or five people, depending on the size of your office and the breakdown of the workflow.

Once a rough draft of this file has been created, the staff person can submit it for review by the entire staff or by you alone. The next step is to make changes based on the review to come up with the final master checklist.

The "Checklist in Action" Approach

If you decide to create the steps of a master checklist by using the "checklist in action" approach, you write the protocol (non-substantive activity) for opening and closing the file based on how that file is typically opened and closed and delegate the task of writing the protocol. Next, have all relevant team members keep a yellow pad on their desk and jot down notes as they work through the file. Instruct them to accumulate all the notes into a draft. Lastly, review the draft with your staff and incorporate any changes to create the final master checklist.

No matter which approach is used, once the master checklist is approved, it should be put on the computer and into a binder with any other explanatory material. At that time, copies of the checklist should be attached to the inside flap of each file as it is opened. Some staff clip it on; some staple it in. It is a permanent fixture on the file, and everyone in the office uses it. The checklist then becomes an up-to-date snapshot of all the work currently done on the case.

Add Options within the Checklist System

Once your master checklist is in use, you may want to add items to the list. For example, a focus on client service and/or referral sources can be built right into your system. Here are some prompts you might include:

- Keep clients updated on the status of their case through preemptive phone calls and/or update letters.
- Tour clients through the office and introduce them to the people they will be working with.
- Give referral sources a thank you (by phone or in writing) and updates when appropriate.

When your systems are built not only around speed and efficiency but specifically around serving your clients well, then everyone benefits. Often clients cannot judge the quality of your work product, but they can tell if you care about them by the way that you or your office keep in touch.

Evaluate and Measure the Success of the System

A checklist should be considered an ever-changing document. There will always be improvements that you can make. When a new checklist is put into use, it will contain some mistakes and some omissions. The job of the people who are using the checklist is to catch those mistakes, fill in any information that has been omitted, and generally upgrade the list. Of course, any new versions should be posted in the appropriate computer directory and an updated copy inserted in the binder. Versions can be created as they are updated so the latest copy of the checklist is always available.

A checklist is not working if it complicates your process. Here are three criteria by which you can measure the success of your checklist system:

- Streamlines the process and eliminates extra steps
- Eliminates guesswork about what is to be done next
- Creates peace of mind that no details are overlooked.

When you have a checklist system in place, your speed is increased, your profits go up, and your clients are pleased with your turnaround time and the accuracy of your information.

Boost Your Checklist Time Savings with a Model Folder

In combination with the checklists, we suggest creating a model file—an example of how you want your files to be organized. It is helpful to use pocket files or multi-partition files and designate which areas of the files are to be used for certain types of documents. For example, the checklist would always be in the front of the file, and the documentation would be placed in agreed-upon locations throughout. This way, when you or your staff pick up a file, you can immediately refer to the checklist to see the status or find the backup documentation you might need.

Establish an Action-Oriented Filing System on Your Desk

The second aspect of systemizing your office is to institute an action-oriented filing system for processing the paper that comes across your desk on a daily basis. As mentioned previously, with the introduction of the personal computer, it was generally believed that we would all be operating in the paperless office well before the year 2000. Yet researchers today say that we are dealing with 10 times more paper than when this prediction was made. Our attorney clients on average lose six weeks a year trying to retrieve information from paper-laden desks and misplaced files.

For most attorneys, the time loss is probably greater. It is not unusual for the attorneys who seek our help to have piles of files on their desks and their credenzas, with more boxes of files on their floors. A client once dropped by unexpectedly to see one of these disorganized attorneys. She had never been to his office before, as he always met with clients in the conference room. Stunned with the mess she walked into, she remarked that she didn't know he was getting ready to move. He was ashamed to admit that he wasn't, and soon after, he called us for help.

With the tremendous influx of paper that comes at you in the mail, from the fax machine, the copier, and your computer's printer, it can be a daunting task to organize it all. The most important pieces of paper generally are attended to, but the rest get stacked, shoved aside, stored away, or pushed out of sight.

An advisor we know referred to attorneys who pile their desks with files as having an "Everything Out" personality. Lacking a filing system that they feel confident in, these attorneys store their files where they can see them. This gives them the false confidence that they will not forget anything. Piles of files are created and distributed according to their importance. Each individual attorney has his or her own formula, but usually the more important the file, the more prominently it is displayed. This means the urgent files sit on the desk and the less time-sensitive items are relegated to the floor, gaining urgency with every hour that passes.

So if filing systems are personality-driven, what would an "Everything Away" personality look like?

For starters, these attorneys put things away because they have trust in their filing system. A clean desk usually indicates a well-organized filing system. All files that are not currently in use are either stored away in a holding file in their desk or credenza or given to their staff to file in the outer office.

These attorneys rely on the calendar and to-do list to tell them what to work on. Because they follow their time template conscientiously, they have faith that they will touch on all important files in their case status review meetings and weekly planning session. Every night before leaving the office, they stop a few minutes early and clear their desks. It takes discipline, staff support, and a good system to operate in this way, but it is possible to see the top of your desk.

It's Time for a Paper "Triage"

When we examine the phenomenon of the "Everything Out" attorneys closely, we discover that piles are a function of three things:

- **Lack of a destination:** Not having institutionalized stations for paper as it is being processed
- **Indecision:** Not deciding on what to do with a piece of paper immediately
- **Horizontal paperwork storage:** Storing paperwork in piles greatly restricts access to a file's contents.

One solution is to stand your files on end to enable you and the staff to **triage** incoming paperwork. By triage, we mean determine the priority for treatment of each piece of paper. This is an inbox on steroids that can be used to process incoming mail, faxes, computer printouts, and any other papers that come across your desk. This solves the destination problem and the horizontal storage problem.

This standing inbox should be placed where you can comfortably use it without getting up. The staff should also be able to access it easily. It should contain four files that open at the top, which are set in a standing file folder stand:

1. Hot file
2. Delegation file
3. Holding file
4. Reading file

The first file is the **hot file,** which can be color-coded with red or orange. This file will contain the high-priority, truly urgent, deadline-driven paperwork that you must deal with immediately. When the staff needs you to address paperwork of any kind, it goes into this file, appropriately flagged. When you are opening mail, the items requiring immediate action go into this file. To ensure that nothing is overlooked, you should be in the habit of touching this file frequently throughout the day. This hot file setup eliminates what would otherwise have been lots of urgent paperwork sitting in random order or, worse yet, buried in a pile somewhere. With this method, all of the urgent items are centralized into one easy-to-access spot.

The next file is the **delegation file**. Into this file go the items that you delegate to the staff. In the section titled "Practice Delegation," we go into detail regarding the use of the delegation file. We will just mention here that you need to set up a delegation file for each staff member to whom you delegate. Upon receipt of paperwork that must be delegated, attach a Post-It Note or, in some cases, a delegation form to direct the staff as to what action is to be taken: "call this person back," "pay this invoice," etc. (See the "Practice Delegation" section for further details and an example of a delegation form.) Specifically, it is a form that enables you to indicate details regarding date due, priority level, and other helpful information. When you hold a meeting with that person, this file folder is ready to go. Or you can keep the items in the delegation file until you are ready to delegate them individually. There is now a station for this category of paperwork, and several more piles are eliminated.

If you rely upon the to-do list function in your case management software and you have access to your staff to-do lists, you can easily post your delegated items electronically. However, most staff members need more information than is provided by the simple posting of a task. In this case, combine a meeting with the staff person to explain the tasks and answer any questions.

The next file is the **holding file**. This file holds all the items that are lower-level priorities—important but not time-sensitive. Paperwork should not linger here too long. This file should be checked on a weekly basis to see that the items within have been dealt with. Block time on your calendar to handle this weekly ritual.

The final file is the **reading file**. This file contains reading material, seminar notifications, bar publications, and the like. We recommend scanning publications and pulling out the articles that interest you, instead of the entire publication, to store in this file. If that seems sacrilegious to you, another method is to drop these publications into your briefcase for reading on the go.

We also mention another important file in this paperwork triaging process: the often underused **circular file,** or wastebasket. Be ruthless here. Force yourself to toss out paperwork that is redundant or can be reproduced if you absolutely have to get another copy in the future. These days, you do not have to save every issue of that trade journal, because you can go online in many cases and download any article that you need—when you actually need it.

Using your new paperwork triage process, you should be able to work in a more organized fashion, especially when you pair this system with the discipline of cleaning your desk every evening. Even more effective is the idea of having a staff person "sweep" your desk once or twice a day. For some attorneys, opening the mail with their assistant keeps them from creating piles, and they immediately hand off the items to be delegated to the assistant to distribute. For others, meeting with their assistant every morning to go through the piles on their desk is an effective way to keep it clean.

When you are truly organized, you'll be able to walk into your office each morning and sit at a clean desk. You will feel much more in control of your practice when you don't have to face piles of files every day.

Merely having the systems in place does not ensure that they will be used. Leadership on your part is the key to their effectiveness when you stress the importance of completing checklists and working with your desktop filing system.

There is no substitution for the feeling you get when you begin getting your office systemized with just these three solutions (checklists, model folder, and paper triaging/standing inbox system) in place. You will have peace of mind and you *will* get positive feedback from clients, referrals, and staff.

Chapter 7

Proactive Strategy Seven: Manage Interruptions

You'll never be able to successfully implement the time template we've just described unless you develop a proactive approach to managing interruptions. In this chapter, we present preemptive strikes for avoiding interruptions altogether, give you some tips for handling them, and help you identify the sources of the interruptions in your office.

Industrial engineers have determined that the average length of an interruption is seven minutes, and it takes about three minutes to get back into what you were doing when you were interrupted. This adds up to 10 minutes per interruption. Six interruptions occur and you have lost an hour; 12 interruptions and you've lost two hours. Many attorneys experience 20 or more interruptions on an easy day.

Many attorneys don't start serious production until after five in the afternoon, when the office quiets down and they can concentrate. They work from five o'clock until eight, nine or later, all the while feeling bad about not spending time with the family or pursuing life outside their practice. It is not uncommon for us to hear attorneys say they view Saturdays and even Sundays as a real haven—not for rest and relaxation, but to concentrate and get work done. When they analyze this statement, they realize it is primarily because there are no interruptions to deal with. However, what they have gained in time spent on production is a huge loss in the personal column of life, interacting with family as well as taking care of themselves. Attorneys who operate this way must then squeeze their so-called personal life into the few hours that remain of the weekend—that is, if they have the energy. Is it any wonder that the failure rate of attorney marriages is so high?

Create Critical Interruption Criteria

Maybe 20% of the interruptions you experience are valid, time-sensitive, and truly important enough to displace whatever you are working on. The remaining 80% of the interruptions can and should be handled at other times and in structured ways. Two proactive methods to help you get a handle on the interruptions in your office are as follows:

- Create standards for what *truly* constitutes a valid interruption during your production time.
- Create a list of allowable interruptions.

"The average American worker has 50 interruptions a day, of which 70% have nothing to do with work."
—W. Edward Deming

Start by creating, with your staff, a list of typical client crisis or emergency scenarios that get your attention when and if they occur. This is a very useful list to help staff distinguish the real emergencies from the false ones. Staff members who are new and not seasoned may believe that every client problem must be immediately elevated to the attorney instead of tactfully handing the client over to the designated hitter, who may be able to help. This is especially true of a new staff person who has never worked in a law practice before and doesn't realize the emotional instability of some clients, who often want extra attention or just someone to talk to. A discussion of real emergencies you have dealt with in the past can be very valuable. We are not trying to downplay the validity of the problems the client may be having; sometimes the client can be satisfied only by talking to you. Sometimes you must immediately respond to something that the opposing counsel, a judge, or a partner has done. There are plenty of legitimate emergencies among those masquerading as such. It is important for you and your staff to clarify the difference. The interruptions at issue are those that can be diverted so that you have protected time for production during the day and not after hours.

Set Criteria for What Constitutes an Emergency

Another way to establish guidelines regarding emergencies and interruptions is to make a list of "allowable interrupters." Your spouse and some family members are usually on the list of people who may interrupt your production time if they have something urgent to discuss. If you have school-age children, the schools should be able to interrupt with urgent messages. You can institute a standing list for your staff and include your spouse, your children's schools, a couple of trusted friends, and even some A+ clients. Some offices make a changing list on a daily basis, which they e-mail or instant message to the call screener. For example, the call screener knows that your spouse and certain other individuals can always get through; otherwise, today's list of allowable calls is limited to those whose files you are currently addressing in your production time. So if you are going to be working on the Smith file and the Jones file today, Mrs. Smith and Mr. Jones are allowed to interrupt. Other than that, you may have a small list of important clients or influencers who get your attention whenever they call. This list should be small and select.

Case Study
Time Management Issue: Handling Emergency Interruptions

Attorney: Divorce Attorney
State: New York

This matrimonial attorney provides us with a great example of handling certain interruptions. One morning, she was in court on a case that went on longer than she'd anticipated. It finally concluded at noon. She had long planned to drive to Amherst, Massachusetts, that afternoon to attend an important event with her family. Scheduled to leave her office for the trip at 1:00, she planned on going home, packing, and then getting on the road by 2:00. Before her departure, however, a long-standing client came in with an emergency that involved the welfare of a young child. All at once, she put her plans on hold, sat down with the client, calmed her, and discussed the appropriate legal action to take. Weighing all of her options, she decided to complete as much work as she could before she got on the road and promised the client she'd continue working on the case during the day via cell phone.

By this point, her schedule was thrown totally off and continued to get worse. She was stuck in heavy traffic and arrived just as the event was ending, much to the disappointment of her family. Instead of the relaxing family gathering she'd planned, her day was filled with stress, frustration and disappointment.

Atticus Tip:
There is no way to schedule every moment and avoid being faced with authentic emergency interruptions at times. This attorney had done it all right: she'd scheduled time to spend with her family, allowed time for the court appearance in case it ran late, and given herself some margin back at the office before she set out on her drive. She never planned, however, to deal with such a time-consuming interruption. On this day, she had to make

difficult choices and pushed her own interests aside in favor of the client's. At times, this is the appropriate choice. The important thing is this: Make this type of scenario a memorable event that you can learn from, and not a typical routine in your office. If you find yourself routinely making choices that further your client's interests and fail to take care of your own, you will begin to resent your clients and despise the practice of law. Try to preempt client crises as much as possible, and begin to overestimate the time needed to accomplish your daily goals so you can absorb the unexpected.

To begin to get a handle on managing interruptions, let's break them down into categories:

- Family and friends who drop by or call
- Office socializing
- Staff, partner and client interruptions
- The "self-interrupting" work style

Handling Interruptions from Family and Friends

Interruptions that may come from your personal life—kids, family or friends—can be managed. The solution lies in redirection.

- Let personal callers know not to call during your production time.
- Direct (or have your call screener direct) personal callers to call during your lunch hour if you plan to eat at your desk.
- Direct your call screener to ask callers if you can call them back after your production time.

Just as you can retrain your staff and co-workers to support your efforts in managing your time, you can let important people in your personal life know that you are trying to be more efficient during the day so that you have more time to be with them in the evenings and on the weekends.

Handling Socializing and Work Interruptions

Let's begin by giving you some quick tips for preempting or shortening socializing and work interruptions. It may be as simple as adopting a new set of nonverbal clues, shifting your body language, or simply making a change in the physical setup of your office. Notice that these tips for "taming" interruptions apply to both work and social situations, as the circumstances causing an interruption inevitably overlap.

- **Use a Visual Cue**
  One attorney we know keeps a photo of his family on his desk. This attorney, because of his warm nature, has been plagued with co-workers who take up a lot of his time discussing their personal problems. Since becoming aware that he is spending a lot of time in unproductive conversation, he has established a quick trigger to remind himself of his goals. He looks at the co-worker, looks at the picture of his kids, and asks himself, "Would I rather spend time talking to this person and end up working late, or see my kids before they go to bed tonight?" Without fail, he chooses the kids. This has been a great source of motivation for him.

- **Let's Do Lunch**
  Corral co-workers to join you for lunch. You are preempting social interruptions by catching up on each other's news and adding a bit of fun and relaxation as well.

- **Tell Them You Prefer E-mail**
  E-mail offers a great alternative to face-to-face and phone conversations because you can answer when it is convenient for you. Internal e-mail is also a great way for staff to batch questions, which you can answer at your convenience.

- **Get Creative with Your Communication Methods**
  Conference calls are great for group communication. One hour spent communicating with a group of three beats three hours communicating one message to three people. Most telephone companies have extended conference-calling services available. One such service, called a bridge line, allows you to put up to 150 people on the same call at the same time. The approach can be useful for much smaller groups as well, especially for meetings that may not warrant travel but involve critical participants from different locations.

  The low-tech method of communicating by memo is a timesaving device as well. It allows you to put all of your thoughts down in a coherent fashion, which can then be sent to as many people as necessary. This leverages your time by allowing you to communicate to many people simultaneously.

- **Let Your Body Do the Talking**
  When you see someone entering your office with whom you do not want to get into a long conversation, stand up. This cues them in a

nonverbal fashion that you are in a hurry or on your way out. If that doesn't slow them down, actually walk toward the door and leave (even if you just walk to the restroom). In addition, when you want to end a conversation, break off eye contact with the other person. They will feel that it is time to leave without you having to say a word.

- **Play Musical Chairs**
  Move the visitors' chairs in your office away from your desk when you are not seeing clients. Make your office a little less comfortable for chatting. When the chairs are not conveniently placed at your desk, people are more likely to stand, and consequently their time with you becomes shorter.

- **Don't Catch Their Eye**
  Move your desk so that you are not in view of the passing traffic in the office. If people can easily see you and catch your eye, they are more likely to come in and socialize.

- **Close Your Door and Mean It**
  Enroll your staff in the idea that when you shut your door, you are not to be disturbed by anyone (except for those on the list). This is critical to your production time. If the rest of the office does not respect your closed door, send out a memo saying that you are committed to managing interruptions so you can be more productive. Mention that your secretary can help anyone in the office who needs to speak to you (unless it is a *true* emergency). As you begin to take your time seriously, so do others. Example 7-1 is a sample of a closed-door policy you could issue in the form of a memo.

EXAMPLE 7-1: MEMO ON CLOSED-DOOR POLICY

In an attempt to manage my time better and concentrate on high-priority projects, I'll be closing my door every day between the hours of 9:00 and 11:00 a.m., starting immediately. During this time, I won't be seeing anyone or taking any incoming phone calls; all incoming calls will be returned between the hours of 11:00 and 12:00 so that clients are taken care of quickly. *(If you have an assistant or designated hitter in place, you can mention that they will be handling the calls at this time.)*

This new schedule will help me eliminate the late nights and weekends I have spent trying to get caught up. If you have questions for me, we can meet before or after my production time or you may e-mail them to me at any time.

Thanks for your cooperation.

- **Tame the Telephone**
  The telephone can be a major source of interruptions. Practice good time management on the telephone by using the following tips:

  - When initiating a call that you want to keep short, set up the expectation that the conversation will be a quick one right from the start:
    "Hi, Dan, I only have a moment, but I wanted to give you quick call about . . ."
    "Hi, Karen, I know you're busy, but I just wanted to give you a quick call to let you know that . . ."
  - When receiving a call that you want to keep short, you can also set up the expectation at the beginning that it will be brief:
    "Hi, Joe, I was just on my way out . . ."
    "Hello, Jane. Unfortunately, I've only got a minute to talk. What can I help you with?"

Statistics show that socializing accounts for 80% of unnecessary interruptions. If you view this in terms of loss of production and loss of personal time, you begin to view the problem as one that needs to be dealt with, not just regarded as annoying. Human beings are social animals, and socializing is important on many levels. It is unrealistic and unhealthy to eliminate socializing altogether. The strong internal rapport and sense of teamwork that a well-run office possesses is built and maintained this way. By adopting the quick tips listed above, you are becoming proactive in a way that results in a work environment in which office socializing is valued but is not intrusive or a constant distraction.

Handling Staff, Partners, and Client Interruptions

Work-related interruptions can come from many sources. We focus on the three sources that are the most problematic: your staff, your clients, and (if you have them) your partners.

Staff-Related Interruptions

Lurk and blurt: One of the major causes of work-related interruptions is staff members who do not feel they have enough time with you to get their questions answered. We touched on this in chapter 6, where we emphasized how important it is to schedule a regular time for your staff to meet with you. In lieu of a regularly scheduled meeting time, your staff will interrupt you because they perceive that you are too busy or distracted to meet with them.

They've stooped to the "lurking and blurting" technique to be able to get the information they need so that they can move on with their task. This means they lurk outside your office door and rush in saying, "I just have to ask you one quick question," or "I just need five minutes of your time." These interruptions are never as quick and easy as you or they like to believe, and they can derail you dramatically. It is not fair to either you or your staff to work like this. Nevertheless, most offices run on the lurking and blurting concept. We encourage you to eliminate that behavior if it exists in your office, because it disrespects your time—the most expensive time in the office—and weakens the time template system.

"Remember the plate-spinner on the old Ed Sullivan Show? I'm him. That's how I feel with all the cases I am juggling, constantly running back and forth just trying to give everything enough of a spin to keep it from crashing to the floor."
—Atticus client

Solution: You can solve this problem by giving staff a reliable meeting time, institutionalized on your time template and theirs, and sticking to it faithfully. If you follow the three-part formula for your production time block, you always meet with staff right before or right after your session behind closed doors. Reinforce the idea of batching, explaining that a batched group of 10 questions presented in one sitting may eliminate 10 interruptions during the course of the day. Also, stick to your commitment to batch your questions for them for the same reasons.

I can't do this without you: The second reason your staff may be a source of constant interruptions is that they are untrained and truly don't know how to do anything in the office without your constant supervision.

Solution: You can solve this problem by providing more training for your staff. If you don't have the time to train them yourself, assign someone else to do it. If you don't have anyone else who can train them, send them to seminars for paralegals and legal assistants. Give them books or tapes. Even if some of the materials are meant for attorneys, your staff may be able to glean some helpful information from them.

You may run into a situation in which a staff person cannot be trained despite your most valiant efforts. We suggest you replace this individual with an experienced person. One of the worst things that a very busy attorney can do is to hire a staff person who knows absolutely nothing of the attorney's practice area just because he or she is inexpensive. These individuals require a significant investment of time and training early on to see if they are even going to be an asset to the firm. When you are extremely busy or know that you can't take the time to train a new hire, do yourself a favor and hire staff with at least a medium level of experience so you don't have to watch every move they make. You save yourself in time what it would have cost you to get an inexperienced hire up to speed.

Client-Related Interruptions

Your clients are another common source of interruptions, but they don't have to be. Look at the following list of challenges attorneys typically encounter and examine the solutions that reduce these interruptions:

Just a quick question: Your clients call you constantly with "quick" questions or because they need "handholding." Every day, you spend hours on the phone reassuring clients and not necessarily discussing substantive matters.

Solution: Use your first client meeting to clarify information about your schedule and office protocol for the best way to contact you, including:

- The time of day you are most likely to be reached
- When you are usually in court (if applicable)
- The name and contact information of your "designated hitter"

A word of caution: It is best to avoid giving clients too much access to you by giving out your home phone or cell phone number. It is aceptable and understandable at times to give these numbers out when you have a true emergency situation, but if you give them out on a regular basis, people subvert your production time by calling you on your cell phone. They track you down after hours with questions that could easily wait until business hours. Try not to contaminate your personal time with unfettered access. You'll eventually resent your clients for invading your privacy and feel even more enslaved by your practice.

Of all of these preemptive strikes against interruptions, using a designated hitter is the most advantageous way of eliminating many interruptions. We talked about the designated hitter's importance in determining the success of the time template in chapter 6. Here, we continue to emphasize the role of the designated hitter when you are trying to conquer the problem of interruptions.

If you can get the designated hitter to bond with the client, most of the questions will go to the designated hitter, not to you. Anything that the designated hitter does not know the answer to, or cannot legally answer, can be brought to your attention, and you can get back to the client or, better yet, the designated hitter can relay your response to the client. In this way, you have included another friendly face in the access chain, and it frees you up from a considerable number of phone calls and face-to-face meetings.

Stop! I'm in crisis!: These folks are probably the ones who showed up at your office, already in crisis, wanting you to drop everything and take care of them immediately. These are the individuals who have probably used two or three attorneys before you. Once you have taken on these clients, you find that your practice is drawn into constant crisis mode along with them.

Solution: Take a proactive stance and be very selective about the clients you take on, as we discussed in chapter 5. You may need to review the key points concerning client selection and view it through the perspective of its usefulness in limiting or eliminating interruptions. Don't revert to being reactive and work with any client who shows up on your doorstep. When a new client is sitting before you, really evaluate whether he or she is likely to cause constant crisis. You can preempt a lot of interruptions, potential chaos, and emotional upheaval in your office by not taking these people on. If you are ever in doubt about whether a potential client is a C- or D-level client, consult with your staff. They can spot bad clients from miles away.

Partners who "lurk and blurt" can be tamed: You may also have interruptions in the form of a partner, or partners, who barge into your office at all times with questions or comments, oblivious to the fact that you are trying to concentrate. They may be trying to discuss important staffing issues, address administrative problems, or simply want to use you as a sounding board for an idea. These partners are showing symptoms of a shortage of reliable meeting time with you to get their questions answered and to discuss important issues. They may have stooped to the "lurking and blurting" technique just to get time with you. In our experience, many firms are managed in a completely ad hoc fashion by two or more partners who have no structured partners' meeting.

Solution: Give your partners a reliable meeting time. Create a once-a-week or twice-a-month partner's meeting. Make attendance mandatory. Institutionalize it in your time template and in theirs, and stick to it faithfully. Teach them to batch their questions and organize a standing agenda that devotes time to the following areas:

- Finance/bookkeeping issues
- Staffing issues, firing and hiring

- Administrative/technology issues
- Marketing plans

Look at Example 7-2, which shows a meeting agenda containing these areas that can assist you and your partners in making meeting time productive. Complete and distribute this form at least 24 hours prior to the meeting to allow partners sufficient time to prepare. Many firms that we work with have a partner's lunch on Monday after a morning meeting with the bookkeeper.

EXAMPLE 7-2: PARTNERS' MEETING AGENDA

Agenda Items	Notes
1. Finance (include bookkeeper when appropriate) ❑ Review Dashboard and/or A/R, A/P, P&L reports ❑ Discuss collection issues ❑ Discuss cashflow projections for upcoming month, quarter ❑ Discuss productivity, timekeeping, bookkeeping, billing issues ❑ Approve large purchases, monitor budget variances ❑ Other:________ ❑ Action items:________ Who:________ By when:________ ❑ Action items:________ Who:________ By when:________ ❑ Action items:________ Who:________ By when:________	Notes
2. Staffing ❑ Discuss personnel problems, upcoming reviews ❑ Discuss plans to fill open positions, vacation coverage ❑ Discuss training to be conducted ❑ Discuss employee benefits ❑ Other:________ ❑ Action items:________ Who:________ By when:________ ❑ Action items:________ Who:________ By when:________ ❑ Action items:________ Who:________ By when:________	Notes

3. **Client Development**
- ❑ Set monthly marketing goals (include charitable and community sponsorships)
- ❑ Discuss media, advertising or PR opportunities
- ❑ Discuss client service goals, client retention issues
- ❑ Review number of referrals, compare to goal, discuss follow-up actions
- ❑ Other:__________
- ❑ Action items:__________
  Who:__________ By when:__________
- ❑ Action items:__________
  Who:__________ By when:__________
- ❑ Action items:__________
  Who:__________ By when:__________
- ❑ Action items:__________
  Who:__________ By when:__________

Notes

4. **Technology**
- ❑ Discuss hardware, software, phone system, website needs or issues
- ❑ Discuss possible upgrades to hardware or software
- ❑ Review and/or plan technology training needs for staff and attorneys
- ❑ Other:__________
- ❑ Action items:__________
  Who:__________ By when:__________
- ❑ Action items:__________
  Who:__________ By when:__________
- ❑ Action items:__________
  Who:__________ By when:__________

Notes

5. **Administrative/Operations Projects**
- ❑ Review facilities, space-planning issues and concerns
- ❑ Discuss office equipment needs, issues
- ❑ Discuss research on large expenditures, discuss supply problems
- ❑ Discuss policies and procedures issues
- ❑ Other:__________
- ❑ Action items:__________
  Who:__________ By when:__________
- ❑ Action items:__________
  Who:__________ By when:__________
- ❑ Action items:__________
  Who:__________ By when:__________

Notes

Are You a Self-Interrupting Attorney?

We have talked about the annoying and costly interruptions of others, but, like many attorneys, you may be the source of many of your own interruptions. You are most likely to be a self-interrupter if you exhibit some of the characteristics we have attributed to the reactive style of time management.

- Driven by adrenaline
- Have a short attention span
- Driven by deadlines (won't act until up against a deadline)
- Easily bored
- Pride yourself on your ability to multi-task

If you fall into one or more of the reactive-style management categories just listed, you may also find that you can relate to these behaviors as well:

- Not only do you interrupt yourself, but you tend to interrupt others.
- You've gotten out of the habit of focusing your attention for longer than 10 or 20 minutes.
- When you close your door to go into your production time, you feel cut off and isolated from the office.
- You want to do anything but work on the files or documents that you have planned. Instead, you feel a tremendous urge to do something else:
  - Pick up the telephone
  - Look at e-mail
  - Write an e-mail
  - Work on a different file
  - Search the Internet
  - Stare out the window
  - Rearrange your desk
  - Catch up on your reading
  - Consult with your partners
  - Read the newspaper
  - Give more instructions to your staff
  - Get a cup of coffee
  - Get a glass of water

- Take a restroom break
- Get a snack

The seemingly innocent urges in this last list are what resistance looks like. These urges are your habitual ways of operating conspiring against you. Trying to set up new habits of focusing your attention during your production time is challenging. When you close your door, you may feel lonely and cut off from the rest of the office, and crave some outside form of stimulation. You won't be very focused initially, and you'll want to do anything but the files or projects that you have assigned yourself to work on. These feelings are all normal, so don't give in. It is up to you to prevail over the hold your old habits have over you.

Solutions for Self-Interrupters

Keep a legal pad handy. One solution is to keep a legal pad handy when you go into production time. The idea is to have a place to capture all of those thoughts that arise to pull you off track during your power-hour time. As all of these urgent, self-interrupting thoughts pop into your mind, simply write them down. If any of the urges are tasks that you really must do, you have captured them on your legal pad and they are then easily transferred to your to-do list after your production time is over.

Time yourself and take a break. If you notice that you cannot concentrate for longer than 20 minutes, set yourself up to work on a project for 20 minutes, and then take a five-minute break, but stay in your office. Give yourself something to do—a quick phone call, for example. Do not leave your office unless you absolutely have to, because you will get pulled farther off track. After your break, either pick up something else to work on or return to the first task and work for another 20 minutes. During the beginning weeks of committing to your production time, knowing you have a break every 20 minutes will help you. The following week, try to concentrate for 25 or 30 minutes at a stretch. In this way you can train yourself to concentrate for longer and longer periods as you raise the bar each week.

Get creative with ways to focus. Experiment to figure out how you can leverage yourself into action. For example, some of our attorney clients know that they are the bottlenecks for paperwork in the office. They use this knowledge to leverage themselves into focusing. Work that they must review comes into their in-box and stays there for weeks at a time. The staff are frustrated waiting for them to review the work before they can proceed to completion. To resolve this situation, these attorneys use the first hour of their production time to review work. This structured approach gives them confidence that they can keep the staff moving on their assigned tasks. Once the review is done, the attorneys concentrate on their own highest-priority production.

One attorney had difficulty making herself go through her case files to get the work moving. We asked her to bring in her assistant for 45 minutes with the stated goal of sorting through all the files together and identifying the work that could be delegated. She was pleasantly surprised to find that teaming up with another person and discussing each file was a creative and effective way to deal with her resistance to this chore.

Some attorneys prefer to review work in the afternoons between client appointments. The key is to learn creative ways that keep you on task and focused. Look at the backlogged work in your office. Decide whether you need to focus on it more formally, and include it in your production time or some other slot on your time template.

Celebrate your small victories. We've worked with many attorneys with short attention spans who initially resisted the power-hour idea. After improving their ability to concentrate, they cling to their closed-door production time as the most important time of their day. They've learned to honor their commitments to themselves. Commit to yourself that you will develop the ability to focus for longer and longer periods. Reward yourself for keeping your commitments.

Managing the Biggest Interruption of All: The Trial

If you are a trial attorney (skip this section if you do not have a trial practice) and have committed to moving toward a proactive approach to time management, the period of time surrounding a trial will be a true test of your ability to stick to that commitment. In many practices, we have witnessed the trial preparation period and the trial period turn into *one big interruption.* The temptation is strong for adrenaline-driven lawyers and irresistible to those with reactive tendencies. The solution is to stick to a reduced time template. This reduced template includes trial-related tasks put into blocks. Consequently, your office is not turned upside down and you remain focused on the trial as well as steady at the helm of your practice responsibilities. Examples 7-3 and 7-4 set forth trial time templates, Option A and B, to give you some guidance on creating one in your practice.

EXAMPLE 7-3: SAMPLE TRIAL TIME TEMPLATE—OPTION A

This modified time template is to help you organize your time in trial, while still tending to the important issues pending with other clients. It allows for an early-morning meeting with your staff to handle trial delegation and non-trial-related client updates. After your day in court there is time for returning phone calls to the most important non-trial-related clients. The day after trial (we have four days pictured; your actual trial may be longer or shorter) is scheduled as a "Phantom Day." This day allows for some recovery time. No client appointments or outside phone calls are scheduled on this day. The attorney is in the office only to catch up on work that has accumulated while in trial.

<table>
<tr><th></th><th>MONDAY</th><th>TUESDAY</th><th>WEDNESDAY</th><th>THURSDAY</th><th>FRIDAY</th></tr>
<tr><td>9:00 a.m.</td><td>STAFF MEETING</td><td colspan="4">MORNING STAFF MEETING PRIOR TO COURT</td></tr>
<tr><td>10:00 a.m.</td><td colspan="4" rowspan="8">APPROXIMATE
TIME IN COURTHOUSE
(THIS TIME WILL BE SHORTER OR LONGER DEPENDING ON THE ACTUAL DURATION OF THE TRIAL)</td><td rowspan="8">PHANTOM DAY</td></tr>
<tr><td>11:00 a.m.</td></tr>
<tr><td>12:00 p.m.</td></tr>
<tr><td>1:00 p.m.</td></tr>
<tr><td>2:00 p.m.</td></tr>
<tr><td>3:00 p.m.</td></tr>
<tr><td>4:00 p.m.</td></tr>
<tr><td>5:00 p.m.</td></tr>
<tr><td>6:00 p.m.</td><td colspan="5">LATE AFTERNOON MEETINGS/
RETURN NON-TRIAL-RELATED PHONE CALLS</td></tr>
</table>

EXAMPLE 7-4: SAMPLE TRIAL TIME TEMPLATE—OPTION B

As this trial begins on Tuesday, it allows for a weekly planning session on Monday and a staff meeting prior to a full day of preparation. While in trial, an early-morning meeting with your staff to handle trial delegation and non-trial-related client updates is scheduled. After your day in court there is time for returning phone calls to the most important non-trial-related clients. The day after trial (we have three days pictured; your actual trial may be longer or shorter) is scheduled as a "Phantom Day" to allow for some recovery time. No client appointments or outside phone calls are scheduled on this day. The attorney is in the office only to catch up on work that has accumulated while in trial.

	MONDAY	TUESDAY	WEDNESDAY	THURSDAY	FRIDAY
9:00 a.m.	STAFF MEETING	MORNING STAFF MEETING PRIOR TO COURT			
10:00 a.m.	TRIAL PREP	APPROXIMATE TIME IN COURTHOUSE (THIS TIME WILL BE SHORTER OR LONGER DEPENDING ON THE ACTUAL DURATION OF THE TRIAL)			PHANTOM DAY
11:00 a.m.					
12:00 p.m.					
1:00 p.m.					
2:00 p.m.					
3:00 p.m.					
4:00 p.m.					
5:00 p.m.					
6:00 p.m.	RETURN PHONE CALLS	LATE AFTERNOON MEETINGS/ RETURN NON-TRIAL-RELATED PHONE CALLS			

Resist the Reactive Approach When Preparing for Trial

The reactive approach is not an uncommon approach among attorneys who have something of an adrenaline addiction. It is caused by knowing that if you wait long enough, you can rely on the adrenaline boost to carry you through those final days and nights of intense preparation. That's when you lock yourself away—eating, sleeping, and thinking of nothing other than the case. You eventually emerge, bleary-eyed, to go forth and try the case. If you win, this whirlwind preparation style is dramatically reinforced. If you lose, you vow to never do it again, and then quite often do. The cycle continues even though you end up hating yourself for this reactive and repetitive behavior.

"Time flies. It's up to you to be the navigator."
—Robert Orben

Proactively Plan and Schedule

Some of your trial preparation has to wait until the last minute, when you are certain the trial really will happen. However, it is possible to jump-start the process. Take those items that can be worked on early and either schedule yourself or someone else to begin working on them. Your proactive approach includes two main goals:

- Anticipate what you need well in advance, and
- Block time early to prepare for it.

Create a Trial Notebook

Three weeks before a trial is not too soon to begin anticipating what you need. One of the critical elements of this preparation is the **trial notebook**. Ideally, you already have a systemized approach to putting a trial notebook together. If not, you can use the notebook for your current trial as the model for notebooks in the future. If you use word-processing software, file your table of contents checklist on your computer for future use.

A systemized trial notebook includes a checklist, a diagram of a notebook, or an actual model notebook to use as reference. You or your staff member can create a detailed table of contents listing every form and document that is typically used. All of your tabs are standardized based on your table of contents and can be made up ahead of time. This detailed table of contents can serve double-duty as the notebook assembly checklist. You can have a staff member begin assembling the notebook so that you can begin filling it up early in the process. Get as much help as you can to start putting the trial notebook together early so that all the work doesn't have to happen the week before trial.

Block the Time for Trial-Related Events

Once your trial notebook has been set in motion, focus on blocking time for all things related to the trial. If you do not block time for it on your time template and your calendar, you will be tempted to bump other work for trial-related activities. Because a fair amount of preparation must occur the week before or several days before the trial, you should try to dedicate all of your production time on those days to trial preparation. Below is a chronological list of activities that should occur as soon as the trial date is set:

1. Block out the trial and several days prior on your calendar.
2. Work backwards and start blocking additional preparation time.
3. Block the day after the trial as a "Phantom Day for recovery."

Staff should automatically block out the days prior to the trial on the calendar to ensure your ability to focus. Have them schedule time by working backwards and blocking additional preparation time up to three weeks before the trial. When lawyers prepare for trial, they go into "hyper-focus" mode. They go behind closed doors, don't allow any interruptions, and really concentrate. We encourage the intensity of this mode, but not the drama and irritability that surround it when it is crammed into the week before trial. Negative feelings result when you become cranky and irritable with staff members, partners, and clients. The solution is to get into hyper-focus mode prior to the week before trial by scheduling an hour or two each day in the three weeks leading up to the trial.

In the week before the trial, continue to conduct your weekly planning session at the beginning of the week. Continue your daily staff meetings so that you can monitor what is happening in the rest of your practice. Take at least an hour to review work that your staff completes in order to keep the work flowing. During your trial, try to maintain a skeletal version of your time template that includes a quick meeting with staff, either on the phone or in person, on a daily basis. Refer to Examples 7-3 and 7-4 to see how this works.

The day after the trial should be blocked as a "Phantom Day for recovery." This means that clients are not told that you are back at work until the next day. This allows you to return to the office and catch up without any appointments. Some attorneys automatically take the day off after a large trial, anticipating that they will be exhausted. Some take it even further and schedule a massage, a movie, or some other pleasurable activity the day afterward just to have some relaxing downtime. To maximize your recovery, make it an activity that requires no brainpower.

Use your best judgment about how to take care of yourself during this very stressful period. Take proactive control over the preparation process. Your goal is to avoid having everything occur at the very last minute, leaving you feeling overwhelmed when you walk into the courtroom and unable to mentally assimilate all the information you are dealing with.

Count and Analyze Interruptions

Now that you have taken a more in-depth look at the pervasiveness of interruptions in the law office setting, you are probably anxious to make some changes. The first step toward implementing those changes is to analyze your specific office environment. As the saying goes, "You can't manage what you can't measure," so we have provided you with two tools to assist you in counting and analyzing the characteristics of interruptions you encounter:

- The interruption log
- The interruption analysis worksheet

The Interruption Log

First, keep a record of the number and type of interruptions you encounter on the **Interruption Log** (see Example 7-5). Make a copy of the log and place it on your desk. If you are subject to a great number of interruptions, you may need more than one page per day to capture them all. Keep the log for one or two weeks and note the interruptions that occur daily. You may also want to make copies of the log for your staff. Comparing your information with them may help you find a quicker solution in the analysis phase.

Notice that the form is divided into two parts: the top part is for *external* interruptions and the second part is for *self-imposed* interruptions. Those are the interruptions that *you* create. Note how long the interruption was, what the purpose or the subject was, and whether it involved a person, a phone call, or your environment (e.g., checking e-mail because it beeps every time a new e-mail shows up). Rank the importance of this interruption. Was it an A-level emergency that required you to drop everything? Was it a B-level issue that was not time-sensitive and could have been batched and handled at a planned meeting? Was it a C-level interruption, of very little importance other than socializing? If you use this form for one or two weeks to record the sources of your interruptions, you will be surprised at what you discover.

EXAMPLE 7-5: INTERRUPTION LOG

Briefly describe all interruptions. Include phone calls, attorney/staff/personal crises, drop-in visitors/clients, and visual or audio distractions. Keep this log for two weeks. Analyze the results using the evaluation questions provided in Example 7-6, Interruption Log Analysis Worksheet.

External Interruptions

Length of Interruption	Purpose/Subject	Who/What			Importance		
		Person	Phone	Environ	A	B	C

Self-Imposed Interruptions

Length of Interruption	Purpose/Subject	Who/What			Importance		
		Person	Phone	Environ	A	B	C

The Interruption Analysis Worksheet

Once you have kept your Interruption Log for a week or so, you have enough information to begin your analysis by using the **Interruption Analysis Worksheet** in Example 7-6. Make a copy of the worksheet for use in future analyses. The worksheet helps you dissect the information that you collected in your log and determine who or what is habitually interrupting you. If you had your staff participate in the logging of interruptions, you can share information as well. From the analysis, you should begin to see patterns.

- Who or what is responsible for the majority of your interruptions?
- Who or what takes the most time?
- How much time do you spend on interruptions?
- How much time do you want to spend?
- What are some causes and solutions?
- What are you willing to commit to changing?
- What is the big picture regarding interruptions in your firm?

EXAMPLE 7-6: INTERRUPTION LOG ANALYSIS WORKSHEET

1 Review the information you collected on your interruption log. Who are your habitual interrupters? (You may find it helpful to review your findings with other staff members to see if they are experiencing the same type of interruptions.)

____

____

____

2 What else may be occurring in your physical environment that is disruptive: computer alarms, e-mail that beeps, loud noises outside your office?

____

____

____

3 Use this chart to help find solutions for underlying causes of your major interruptions as listed in questions 1 and 2. **Write down as many solutions as you can think of, even if they seem impossible or impractical**, such as I need my attorney/staff to leave me alone, or I need a door!

____

____

____

4 How many hours per day do you spend handling numbers 1 and 2?

____

5 How many hours per day should you spend?

____

6 For the next 30 days, commit to three solutions that are most viable. At the end of 30 days, go back and review your progress. Did you realize a time savings? If so, congratulations! Now, go back to your original log and choose another interrupter to tackle. If one or more of the solutions you chose did not work, reevaluate them using these questions:

- What worked and didn't work?
- Were the solutions reasonable and realistic?
- Are there additional solutions that need to be explored? Should someone else be involved?
- How have others in your firm managed? Can you make their solutions work for you?

Rigorously managing your interruptions by setting criteria, identifying the sources of your major time bandits, and committing to their limitation or elimination are the keys to reclaiming concentration time during your workday. You'll discover that your production time does not have to start at five o'clock when the phones stop ringing and everyone else leaves the office.

Chapter 8

Proactive Strategy Eight: Practice Delegation

In this chapter, we focus on the art of delegation as a strategy for proactive time management. To make the same amount of money or more, yet work fewer hours and have a personal life, you must be able to delegate. The attorney who tries to do it all and minimizes the involvement of other staff members becomes quickly burned out and reduces his or her option to have time away from the practice.

Many of our attorney clients have had bad experiences with delegation in the past, which has led them to believe that they cannot trust anyone else to do their work as accurately or as quickly as they do. This is called the **self-enhancement bias.** In some cases, the decision for the attorney to do a task is warranted. However, there are staff members who outperform their supervising attorneys on certain tasks. It is important to distinguish which tasks require an attorney's special skills and which do not, without bias.

These same attorneys usually have a story about how they gave an assignment to an assistant, a paralegal, or an associate that ended in disaster. What they failed to realize is that often the way they delegated in the past was, in effect, more like *abdication* than delegation. Substantive assignments were probably doled out with little direction, no training, poor support, and no follow-up. Bad things invariably happened as a result.

As we proceed in this chapter, we emphasize specific delegation skills that enhance your chances of success. The ability to delegate depends on your willingness and ability to undertake the following:

- Identify those parts of a case or file that require your special talents, or your law degree, to handle.
- Trust that you can train others to assist you in delivering a high degree of service and care to your clients by embracing the team approach.
- Analyze workflow and identify tasks for delegation.

- Set up a system to track delegated tasks.
- Provide specific training, information, and context to staff and associates when delegating a task.

All of these elements are necessary for true delegation to occur.

Recognize When to Let Go

Are you guilty of holding on to work that really doesn't require a law degree to handle? When working with our attorney clients to determine how leveraged they are, the first indicator that we look at is the ratio of attorney time per file to staff time per file.

$$\frac{\textbf{Attorney time per file}}{\textbf{Staff time per file}}$$

This seemingly simple ratio is what creates leverage, and leverage is what creates profit in a law practice. Your profit margin depends on your ability to deliver the work for less than it cost you to produce it. The attorney who is freed from lower-level production through delegation is able to manage a greater number of files and ultimately generate more revenue with an increased volume of matters. The simple translation is this: The more work that you, the attorney, do on each case, the less profit you are making; the more work you can delegate to team members, the more profit you are making, because you are able to dedicate time to more cases. The ratio varies depending on the type of case or file, but you should look for an average ratio that indicates you are delegating as much as possible.

"I was so busy doing things I should have delegated, I did not have time to manage."
—Charles Percy, President, Bell & Howell, U.S. Senator

To identify those parts of a case that require your special talents or your law degree to handle, you need to review typical case files. You can determine your attorney time per file versus staff time per file by assigning a time estimate to each task that you do and to each task handled by staff. By comparing the total time you spend on the file with the total time staff spends on the file, you'll get your ratio.

This is easier to do if you have a checklist of tasks for each type of file on which you work. If you don't already have a checklist of tasks that you use to direct the activity within each of your typical file types, it is a good idea to create one according to the steps outlined in chapter 6. Exercise 8-1 requires a checklist to analyze. When your checklist is finished, complete the exercise to get some idea of your current delegating habits.

EXERCISE 8-1:
ANALYZE YOUR CURRENT DELEGATING HABITS

Instructions: Complete the following steps.

1. Review your selected checklist.
2. Place a check beside those actions that you typically complete yourself.
3. Place a star next to those actions that you could delegate.
4. Count the number of items that have both a star and a check.

In the exercise, did you find any tasks that you are currently not delegating? Each task you delegate is time you can save. The time you spend reviewing work done by others will increase, but is usually less than if you took on the task yourself. Your "attorney time per file to staff time per file" ratio is improved if you reduce your attorney time and increase the staff's time by delegating these tasks.

Trust Others to Assist You

If you have found that you are not well leveraged, you may now be motivated to delegate more. The next step is developing an attitude of trust. This may be the hardest part of the delegation process. It is a complex issue that is often at the heart of failed delegation attempts. One of the best ways to begin trusting those you should delegate to is to realize that it does not have to be an all-or-nothing situation.

Institute Levels of Trust

Establishing levels of trust among staff and associates gives the attorney some control and peace of mind and empowers the person to whom the task is delegated. Here are some guidelines for the levels of trust and empowerment you may institute in your office as you begin to practice more delegation.

- **Level One:** Bring the facts to me and *I will decide*.
- **Level Two**: Recommend alternatives and *I will decide*. (This is appropriate for the new staff member or associate attorney who is still in training.)

- **Level Three**: *You decide* and report your decision to me. (This level applies to a more experienced team member who has enough judgment and experience to make reasonable recommendations.)
- **Level Four:** *You decide*. No report needed. (This level of empowerment is usually reserved for partners whom you trust implicitly and who operate within clearly delineated areas of responsibility. It can also be used for senior-level staff and associates who have been team members for many years and have proven themselves beyond reproach.)

Further analysis of tasks regarding level of risk, level of complexity, and whether or not the task reoccurs may help with your trust issues regarding delegation.

Case Study
Time Management Issue:
Training Associates to Enhance Delegation Opportunities

Attorney: Mark Chinn
State: Mississippi

Mark's profile of the ideal associate includes candidates with great people skills in addition to their lawyering skills. Depending on the level of experience they possess, associates are given the opportunity to shadow other associates in order to learn Mark's systems. In addition, their work product is reviewed and critiqued. Once a new associate proves capable of handling more complex work, he or she is given the chance to work with clients directly. Mark manages the team through regularly scheduled case status review meetings and quick meetings he calls "huddles."

Atticus Tip
Monitor the growth of new team members and gradually expose them to more and more complex work. Be sure to provide feedback on new associates' work instead of making changes for them. This technique allows them to develop critical thinking skills and better legal judgment.

Establish a Method to Analyze Which Tasks to Delegate

Determining what to delegate to untrained staff or associates is one of the most difficult decisions you face. In this situation, you fear overwhelming them with work that is beyond their abilities and worry that you won't catch their mistakes. When most attorneys are faced with the need to delegate to an untrained staff member and don't have a methodology or a logical way to think about it, they default to doing the task themselves. The rationale is always "I can do it better and faster." Our philosophy is "Just because you *can* do something doesn't mean you *should* do it."

The Risk/Complexity Matrix Task Analysis

One of the reasons many attorneys have the "I'll do it myself" mentality is because they have the tendency to lump all tasks together. They don't stop to analyze tasks to see the differences in complexity or the amount of risk they would encounter if they did delegate. Here we introduce you to a method that can assist you in this analysis. The method is called the **Risk/Complexity Matrix,** from the *Institute of Management and Administrations Law Office Management Report 2000.* With this approach, you can begin to analyze that pile of work sitting on your desk. You may become more inclined to trust others through delegation and begin to work toward a team approach. Here are some examples of risk/complexity scenarios.

- A **low level of risk** would be to assign someone the task of writing a letter. The risk associated with this **simple task** might be the chance that the letter goes out with a grammatical error. This scenario would be embarrassing to you because it does not represent the standards you try to uphold, but in the realm of all the risks you incur just by having a law practice, it is not a fatal error and represents a relatively low level of risk. Your client's case would probably not be jeopardized because of the error.
- A **high level of risk** would be present if you sent a new associate to cover a hearing, **a complex task,** for which he or she was unprepared.

You might be thinking at this point that you should do all the high-risk and complex tasks and should delegate the low-risk and simple tasks. That would be premature, because there is another element in the risk/complexity method of analyzing tasks for delegation. The element is the issue of recurrence.

The Impact of Task Recurrence on Your Decision

If a task is a unique occurrence and it takes you more time to explain it or to train somebody than to do it yourself, then save training (explaining) time and do it yourself. This is true despite level of complexity and level of risk.

If a task recurs again and again in the lifetime of your practice, it is beneficial to invest the time to train another person and delegate the task. This is time well spent, as you recover your time investment every time you delegate the task in the future. This is true despite the level of complexity and level of risk.

However, be careful which tasks you deem unique. Your self-enhancement bias may lead you to believe almost everything takes longer for you to explain than to do yourself. But this is not always true. You sacrifice the long-term benefits of training for the short-term benefit of expediency.

Refer to Example 8-1, Risk/Complexity Matrix, as we discuss the reasoning behind the method.

EXAMPLE 8-1: RISK/COMPLEXITY MATRIX

	Low Complexity	High Complexity
Low Risk	If project is never to be repeated and would take longer to explain: *Do it yourself.* If project is to recur: *Delegate* entire task, leave time to review.	If project is never to be repeated and would take longer to explain: *Do it yourself.* If project is to recur: *Delegate and use as training opportunity.* Break down into small tasks, give instruction, supervise, leave ample time for review and correction.
High Risk	If project is never to be repeated and would take longer to explain: *Do it yourself.* If project is to recur: *Delegate* entire task. Leave time for review and correction.	If project is never to be repeated and would take longer to explain: *Do it yourself.* If project is to recur: *Delegate and use as training opportunity.* Break down into small tasks, give instruction, supervise, leave ample time for review and correction.

High-Risk/Low-Complexity Tasks

If a task has a high level of risk associated with it but a low level of complexity, it is okay to delegate it by giving exact instructions to your staff person and scheduling ample review and revision time because of the high level of risk involved. You want to make sure it is perfect, but because of the low complexity of the job, you do not have to be hands-on with it.

"The conventional definition of management is getting work done through people, but real management is developing people through work."
—Agha Hasan Abedi, President, Bank of Credit and Commerce International

High-Risk/High-Complexity Tasks

If a high-risk/high-complexity task (which **recurs**) can be broken into smaller, less complex chunks that you can delegate, do it. Even if you have to handle the more difficult pieces yourself, use it as an opportunity to train staff. Set a "false" deadline for staff to complete the work and submit it for your review. This action provides you with ample time to address it prior to the real deadline. If the task is unusual and will not recur, and you don't have much time, you are probably better off doing it yourself.

Low-Risk/Low-Complexity Tasks

If the task is not very complex and has a low level of risk, delegate it completely and leave yourself a little time to review it at the end. The simple-letter writing task we mentioned earlier falls into this category.

Low-Risk/High-Complexity Tasks

If the task is low-risk but very complex, break it into chunks, delegate the less-complex chunks to your staff, and do the more complex tasks yourself. Use the explanation time, your review time, and follow-up teaching opportunities. Leave yourself ample time to do each, as this is a complex task/set of tasks.

Use a Designated Hitter as the Core of Your Team

One of the easiest ways to transition to widespread delegation and a full team structure is to start with a "team of two": you and one other person (the **designated hitter)** to whom you delegate. By emphasizing a team approach and slightly de-emphasizing yourself as the primary client contact, you can provide more personalized service to your clients at a reduced cost and with less handholding. This person plays a critical role in those proactive strategies. In this section, we emphasize the importance of this role.

The designated hitter is usually a paralegal who is responsible for assisting the attorney on each case or file and who handles much of the lower-level communication. The ideal candidate for this position is someone who is enough of a technician to handle the legal work delegated to him or her and enough of a "people person" to provide a sympathetic ear to clients. Review your staff to locate someone who has technical skills but also possesses a friendly, caring manner and a positive attitude.

The Duties of the Designated Hitter

Some of the specific duties of the designated hitter include the following:

- Initiates proactive "check-in" and update calls (provides a higher level of perceived client care)
- Handles incoming phone calls from clients (frees the attorney from interruptions, answers client questions, and refers higher-level questions to the attorney for answers)
- Builds rapport with clients (squires them around the office)
- Provides handholding when necessary
- Conducts partial intake interviews on the phone and in person

We have discussed some aspects of the designated hitter's role in earlier chapters. In this section, we focus on the proactive check-in call. We suggest that the attorney delegate the task of calling clients to provide updates and answer questions. We promote this idea because the most frequently cited frustration that clients have with attorneys is lack of accessibility.

The typical scenario goes something like this: The client calls the attorney to ask a question. The attorney is not available. The client is told the attorney will call back or, worse, to call back later. When the attorney and the client finally connect, hours or days later, the client is frustrated from the wait and perceives that the attorney doesn't care about his or her case.

When a client receives a proactive phone call from your designated hitter, the scenario changes:

> "Mr. Attorney asked me to give you a call and check in on you," or "Mrs. Attorney wanted me to call and let you know that . . . ."

The client feels that he or she matters to the attorney. The attorney did not have to take time, other than to delegate the designated hitter to make the call, and the client feels taken care of.

Some of our attorney clients who adopt this practice require the calls to be made on a weekly or monthly basis. Others make individualized assessments of the client's communication needs and plan their calls accordingly.

We call these phone calls **preemptive strikes.** We know that many clients are under extreme stress and may require additional maintenance. While it may sound like a time-consuming idea, it actually saves time to take such preventive measures. When we examine the source of interruptions that attorneys typically endure, handling client crises is at the top of the list. Using a designated hitter to help keep clients from playing phone tag with the attorney and feeling frustrated prevents a great many interruptions. Using preemptive strikes to keep clients informed, even when there is not much to report, helps to reduce the number of client crises.

You can also use the designated hitter to write explanatory letters when copies of relevant documents are sent. Both of these types of preemptive strikes have an extra advantage: Clients are much more likely to pay for your services when they have been kept well informed of your work during the process. When our attorney clients practice delegation combined with enhanced client communication, everyone wins. Clients feel cared for and are more likely to tell others of their positive experience.

Introducing the Designated Hitter to the Client

Because the designated hitter is involved in many aspects of the work you'll do with clients, you should make a formal effort to bring him or her into each new client interaction. The proper way to introduce your designated hitter is to have him or her attend the very first client meeting. This indicates to the new client that your staff member will be very involved in his or her case. In some cases, it is the designated hitter who conducts part of the intake interview, but your job, no matter what the arrangement, is to extend the trust and confidence that the client develops in you to include your designated hitter. This is especially important if the new client is someone who has been referred to you based on your reputation.

You begin this trust-building process by introducing this special staff person in a powerful way. Clients take their cue from you on how to interact with your staff person. It is up to you to endorse the designated hitter and thereby direct client expectations in a positive way. You should never apologize for the presence of a designated hitter and should always present him or her as a trusted staff member who helps you provide a higher level of service.

Here are three scripts that may guide you in the introduction of your designated hitter. The first one comes from one of our attorney clients.

- "We operate as a team in this law firm. Let me introduce you to one of our most valuable players: This is Susan Jones. She'll work with me to make sure you're taken care of. In fact, when I am out of the office or in court, she'll be the one who can answer your questions, so be sure to ask for her when you call."
- "To make sure your needs are met, we have developed a top-notch team. Their job is to make sure you feel taken care of. Let me introduce you to Beth. She'll be working with me, shoulder to shoulder, on your case and will often be more available to answer your questions than I am. Be sure to ask for her when you call. If there is anything she can't help you with, she'll meet with me and get back to you as soon as possible."
- "By the way, her hourly rate is quite a bit less than mine, and we find that we can save our clients money when she answers your questions or helps you when you call."

(Note: This last script refers to a designated hitter's lower hourly rate, which is usually very well received by clients.)

A variation of this approach can be taken with some referral sources who might want to know about clients they have referred. From time to time you may direct your designated hitter to compose a short note on the status of the matter (when ethically appropriate) to keep the referral source in the loop. One of the biggest complaints that referrers have about attorneys is that they feel uninformed about work they have referred. By attending to the communication needs of your referral sources, you ensure that the referrer feels comfortable about sending work to you in the future.

Let's sum up the benefits of this service-oriented approach to using a designated hitter:

- Reduces the number of phone calls the attorney must deal with on a daily basis
- Minimizes the number of client crises that the law office must handle
- Offers more personalized attention to the client, which translates into future referrals

Case Study
Time Management Issue: Paper and Desk Management Systems That Enhance Delegation Opportunities

Attorney: Richard West
State: Florida

Richard West is an attorney in Orlando, Florida. At the writing of this book, he is serving as the chairman of the family law section of the Florida Bar Association. Despite this busy schedule, Richard runs an office that is the closest to being "paperless" that we have seen. He does this with a twofold system. First, all incoming mail is scanned into his computer/laptop by an assistant. Not only does this eliminate a great deal of paper in his office, it allows him to review the mail from remote locations as well.

The second part of his system, which promotes a clutter-free office, is the use of desk management. Critical to the success of his system is the designation of two drawers: an open file drawer and another for frequently used files. He keeps an open file drawer on his desk as a staging area to allow him to clear his desktop quickly by dropping his files neatly back into the open drawer when a client comes in or he has to undertake an unscheduled project. In the other drawer he keeps several specifically designated holding files containing matters that he needs to handle frequently, such as accounts receivable, articles or lectures he is working on, his committee chair lists, and phone numbers. He also keeps a separate file folder for each member of his staff into which he places any documents that he needs to discuss with that staff member. When he meets with staff, he merely reaches for their files to cover all matters at one time.

As a part of this system, any file that he is not actively using is out of his office and filed appropriately. He cleans off his desk at the end of every day so that he is automatically organized for the next day. The credenza is reserved for reference materials that are used on a frequent, or perhaps daily, basis.

For an attorney who must travel a great deal, this is an ideal system that focuses on priorities and taps into the power of good time management.

Track Delegated Tasks

One guaranteed way to create chaos and waste time is to delegate without tracking. Therefore, before delegating anything, we encourage you to set up a tracking system.

The Delegation File Method

The tracking system we recommend can be used alone or in conjunction with case management software to delegate electronically. The system, called the **Delegation File Method**, has several steps that enable you to track and follow up on delegated tasks. It originates with one file designated to each person to whom you delegate. The file activity is tracked through to completion in regularly scheduled meetings. Here are the steps you follow:

1. *Create a delegation file* for each person whom you currently supervise. Set the files up in a vertical file holder within arm's reach. They can be placed on your credenza, bookcase, or on a corner of your desk. Label each file with the name of one person to whom you delegate.
2. *Set up a meeting schedule* that you follow faithfully, for the people to whom you delegate. The easiest way to do this is to meet 15 to 30 minutes prior to your production time. Whenever it is established, it is important to block time for the meeting on your calendar. Instruct staff and associates to do the same.
3. *Use a written delegation form.* When you meet with each person, bring his or her delegation file to the meeting. Use a written delegation form that you fill out for each task delegated. (See Example 8-2, Delegation Form, following Step 4, below.) Review past delegation forms; you can modify ours to suit your needs. Write out what must be done and put a copy of the form into your file for future reference. For even more convenience, have your delegation forms reproduced as carbon-free two-part forms. When you complete the forms and give a copy to your staff member, you have an instant copy to drop in your file. When you return to your office, post the deadlines on your calendar to follow up on the delegated tasks in a timely fashion. You can also make notes in your file folder for the next meeting.

   In the event you use case management software with a task function that allows you to electronically post "to-do's" for your team, work out a method to track their completion. This usually involves assigning a due date.
4. *Review past delegation forms.* At each successive scheduled meeting, pull out the old delegation sheets and review them before delegating new tasks. This way, any tasks that were not followed up on by calendared dates are followed up on in the meeting. This creates a fail-safe way to make sure that tasks don't fall through the cracks.

EXAMPLE 8-2: DELEGATION FORM

Assigned to: ____

Today's Date: ___/___/___ Due Date: ___/___/___

Priority: ❑ A ❑ B ❑ C Grade: ____________________

Instructions: ____

____

____

Please: ❑ run with this task and report back to me upon successful completion

❑ check in with me ❑ daily ❑ weekly ❑ monthly ❑ bi-monthly

I prefer to remain informed via ❑ verbal update ❑ written report ❑ e-mail

The purpose of this task is ______________________________

____

____

This task affects ❑ me ❑ the firm ❑ our client, as follows:

____

____

CONSEQUENCES of failing to handle this request:

____

____

____

Please add this item to your master TO-DO list promptly!

Choose the Correct Training Method to Match Your Need

When you begin to delegate more work to your team, deficiencies in their skills may become more obvious. Issues that may arise include:

- How much training is needed?
- When do I provide training?
- Who needs training?
- What kind of training is needed?

Formalized training (planned ahead, ongoing) for everyone is a great systematic way of addressing all these issues. By patiently providing ongoing training for your team and allowing yourself plenty of focused review time, you can give yourself more peace of mind, save time, and get better results.

Small-firm attorneys who may be short on patience and backlogged with work find it difficult to provide formal training on a regular basis. They often want new team members to "hit the ground running" but won't pay for experienced staff members. Consequently, there is great frustration among the staff as they are pressed into service and lack adequate information about what they are to do.

We encourage you to use every opportunity to train. Instill in your firm a learning culture and infuse it with constant learning opportunities. Here are some ways to work toward these goals:

- Send your team to continuing legal education (CLE) seminars and workshops.
- Buy books and tapes from CLE courses.
- Assign a staff member to "job shadow" another individual.
- Assign a buddy or a mentor to a staff member for one-on-one guidance.

You can also set up a weekly training session for all relevant staff and associates. It is easy to set the training up in the style of a meeting. Everyone gathers around the conference table to autopsy old cases, old files, old matters, and to discuss certain aspects, technical and otherwise, of each case.

Another way to set up a weekly training session is the "lunch and learn" format. Set it up for noontime, mid-week or on Friday. Order a pizza and present, or have an associate or partner present, a topic on which everyone should be trained.

Don't forget to use the case status review meetings as another opportunity for training. Use those meetings to continually teach staff what the next step is in an ongoing case. Make it an interactive exchange in which staff are called upon for ideas and solutions, making them the "presenters." If a staff member brings a problem to your attention in these meetings, request that he or she bring a possible solution as well. This trains your staff to think in a more critical fashion and allows you to measure their critical thinking skills and judgment.

"Perhaps the most valuable result of all education is the ability to make yourself do the thing you have to do when it ought to be done, whether you like it or not."
—Thomas Henry Huxley, Biologist

We promote the idea of formalized training sessions combined with "just-in-time" training. Just-in-time training is everyday, on-the-job training. It occurs every time the attorney takes a little more time to explain the work that he or she is delegating in order to give sufficient information and provide context. It also occurs every time an attorney reviews the work done by associates and staff and makes corrections. This may involve discussing the corrections or having the team member make the corrections. The goal is to have the feedback loop completed and for the person to learn what he or she did wrong. This is the scenario we are trying to avoid: A staff member doesn't understand the task he or she is addressing; the work is submitted to the attorney for approval; the attorney corrects it and fumes about how badly it has been done; the attorney gives no feedback to the staff member. Over time, this attorney tends to delegate less and less.

Every day presents numerous training opportunities to bring staff and associates up to speed. Dividing more complex work into small pieces, which can then be delegated, is a great technique to leverage the attorney's time and to train the staff. In a perfect world, new staff members would be given work that is appropriate for their level of entry, then evaluated as to how well they did. More training would be provided followed by more challenging work, with detailed feedback about their performance along the way. In this way, they are brought up to speed by being offered work that is increasingly complex, with more risk. In the real world, new team members are often slammed with complex assignments within their first week on the job. If the attorney's office is already overwhelmed and not systemized (no checklists or written procedures), the results can be disastrous.

Delegate with Confidence

Once you have practiced the proactive delegation techniques we have outlined, you will begin to see yourself delegate with confidence. As one final reminder, we offer you a summary of how the time template resolves many of the problems with quality control and supervision due to the weekly and daily meetings built into it. To emphasize their importance as a support system for proper delegation and tracking, we'll mention them again with specifics:

- Have small daily **staff/associate meetings** as a forum for giving context to and providing specific instructions for delegated tasks.
- Block time for **training** if required for staff/associates to accomplish tasks.
- Exercise interim quality control in regularly scheduled **case status review meetings**.
- Schedule yourself to **review work** often enough to keep it flowing and for a final review as the last step in your delegation process.

In addition, we have provided an acronym that serves as a quick summary of some delegation rules to keep you on the right track. We use the acronym **SMART Rules for Delegation** because we feel that delegation is the smartest way to approach your workload for efficiency and for profit.

SMART RULES FOR DELEGATION

Specific: If there is a high level of trust and this is a frequently delegated task, you can be less specific. But if this is the first time it is delegated and there is little experience or familiarity, you must be very specific about all the actions to be taken, possibly putting them into written form, depending on the complexity of the task.

Measurable: Establish exactly what you intend for the outcome. If possible, quantify the result. State it clearly and ask for it to be repeated to check for accuracy.

Accountable: Select someone who will take ownership of the project or task. Make it someone who will communicate results in a timely fashion and will not try to cover up or require lots of attention or reassurance.

Realistic: Create checkpoints along the way to check the progress and quality of the work. Allow extra time for mistakes that are part of the initial learning curve—just make sure you have a way to catch them. Don't delegate something that isn't humanly possible to accomplish in a given time frame. Make sure you provide adequate resources to get the job done; if time is short, more assistance may be required.

Timeline: State very clearly the date for completion, any checkpoint dates, and the consequences of not meeting the deadline. Remember that the first time any task or project is undertaken, it will take longer to accomplish. Expect increased efficiency with repetition.

Questions to ask yourself when trying to decide if it is worth delegating a task:

- Does this require *my* special skills?
- Could someone else do this?
- How often will this task be done in the future?

Chapter 9

Proactive Strategy Nine: Take a Vacation

Planning and taking a vacation is the best way to test whether your office is fully systemized, your team is trained, and your practice is capable of running without you.

Leave the office for a period of a week or two and don't call in. If your systems are properly in place and the staff is well trained, you will return to a practice that is not in crisis; business has progressed smoothly and your absence has not been a problem so far as your clients are concerned.

If, on the other hand, you come back and the place is in turmoil, clients are upset because you haven't been there, and two weeks of mail sits unopened on your desk, it probably is a safe bet that you are not fully systemized. We often say that your business "speaks" to you with its breakdowns. Knowing this gives you the opportunity to autopsy any breakdown, large or small, trace it back to its roots, and assess where you need to improve. Although it may seem a remote possibility to you now, it is possible to be away from your office and have it operate smoothly without you. With the proper planning, clients do not have to experience your absence as problematic, mail does not have to pile up unopened, and business as usual can proceed.

Good Reasons to Stay Put?

For some attorneys, the fact that they haven't taken time off in the last decade is a source of pride. In fact, it is not unusual for many of our clients to admit that they have not taken a vacation in 10, 15, or even 20 years!

These attorneys judge themselves only as producers of legal work, not as human beings with a need for recreation. In fact, recreation holds no attraction for them while in the grip of their Puritan work ethic. Often these attorneys work on the weekends and don't make time for their passions, interests or hobbies. These may also be the attorneys who feel disconnected from their family and friends. When questioned about not taking a vacation, their reasons include the following:

- There is never a good time to go away—the court calendar won't let me take time off.
- I can't leave my clients—things would fall apart without me being here.
- My partners don't take vacations and I would feel bad taking one if they haven't.
- I have too much to do around here—maybe I'll go if I ever get caught up.
- It's too much trouble to go away—I have to work twice as hard when I get back to make up the time.
- I'll take an extra day or two when I travel to Bar events and conferences—that's enough travel for me.

There may never be a convenient time to take a vacation. There will always be reasons why you should not leave your practice. We are convinced, however, that with enough advance planning, you can make it work. Planning a vacation far enough in advance enables you to design your life and your practice to make it happen.

Time off may actually benefit your practice. When you leave your environment for a week or two and allow yourself to stop thinking about the technical aspects of your practice (which may not happen until the second week), new and more creative ideas will occur to you. The new perspectives they bring back have surprised many of our attorney clients. But you will never experience this phenomenon if you don't take yourself away from your practice and experience another environment for a while. You owe it to your practice to try this out.

How to Make It Work

One Year to Six Months Out

Block your vacation time on the calendar. By setting your vacation up early, you avoid any problems with the court calendar.

In addition, bookend your trip with a couple of "Phantom Days." Phantom days are those in which you are in the office but don't see any clients or take any outside calls. Clients believe that you are still out of town. Instruct the staff that these are the days you will need to prepare to go away and to catch up when when you return. It is important to get caught up before clients know that you are back. Having these Phantom Days allows you to enjoy the last few days of your vacation without dreading that first-day-back onslaught that would otherwise await you. Once you see how pleasant it can be to return to your practice when you aren't faced with a packed day, you'll never plan a trip any other way. Enlist your staff in this bit of calendaring magic, and don't allow them to sabotage it by scheduling even one small meeting.

Also around this time, line up a backup attorney whom you can trust. If you are a solo practitioner and don't have anyone you can rely upon internally, call among your colleagues. It is not unusual for the solo practitioners with whom we work to have an informal arrangement with another solo practitioner to cover for them in the event of an emergency or a vacation. Failing that, contract with another attorney you trust and have worked with over the years.

Six Weeks to One Month Out

Meet with your team and create a list of client crises that could occur while you are gone. Look at your most volatile client situations and project one month out what might become a problem so that you can preempt any predictable emergencies while you are gone.

Meet with your backup attorney and make sure he or she has all the phone numbers that might be needed and appropriate access to your files. Discuss any case you consider to be unstable and what to do if a breakdown occurs.

In addition, start anticipating what you need from opposing counsel if you have a litigation practice. Unless they are truly adversarial in every way, most will cooperate with you to a reasonable degree. Start making a list of requests you might make of them, and also of the courts, to preempt any negative impact on your clients. Finally, begin telling clients that you will be away next month but are taking measures to see that nothing will interfere with the course of their case. If need be, introduce them to the backup attorney.

Two Weeks Out

Update your list of client concerns and create contingency plans for them. Discuss the list with your backup attorney and with your staff, especially your designated hitter. If you don't have one, schedule the staff to place calls to clients while you are gone. Provide a sample script such as the following:

> Mr. or Mrs. Attorney is out of town for the next two weeks, as you know, but he (she) wanted me to touch base with you and see how

you are doing while he (she) is gone. Do you have any questions or concerns that I can help you with while he (she) is away?

Clients typically are so grateful that they are attended to so well that they don't perceive the attorney's trip as a problem. These calls will also serve as an early-warning system if trouble is brewing among the clientele.

Take this time to get caught up on any outstanding billing so that it is current when you return. Discuss with your bookkeeper how to manage the bookkeeping functions while you are away so that deposits are made and bills go out on schedule.

If you likely will receive referrals during your time away, you can handle them one of two ways: (1) tell your referral sources to hold their referrals while you are away (you can even set appointments with them in advance); or (2) empower your designated hitter or backup attorney to conduct a pre-interview with prospective clients to get them started and into the system. Your staff can show the client around the office, provide your new client information packet and reading material, and assure him or her that you'll hit the ground running when you return (after your Phantom Day). Entrust this task to someone equipped to handle inquiries about your fees in an appropriate manner, and make sure that your intake person is careful not to sign up C- and D-level clients in your absence.

One Week Out

If you don't already have one, create a mail-triaging system. This is a system to categorize and handle mail of all types, from the urgent, high-priority mail (the urgent, time-sensitive category) to correspondence that is not urgent but provides a deadline (non-urgent, time-sensitive category) to reading material that is not time-sensitive at all (non-urgent category).

Do not come back to a desk and chair piled high with unopened mail and a long list of e-mails on the computer. Make sure someone in the office opens both the mail and your business e-mail, identifies any important documents or issues that need to be handled immediately, distributes them to the right people, and categorizes the rest. After such person determines the high-priority items, he or she should set aside the lower-priority mail, grouped into their proper categories, and discard junk mail, or hold it for your review. Depending on the length of time you will be away, you may consider setting up an "auto-responder" to automatically notify each person who e-mails you that you are out of the office.

In the final week, meet one last time with your backup person to ensure that he or she has the latest information to handle any situation that may arise.

Do This for You and Your Practice

The length of vacation time to which this protocol applies is anything longer than three or four days. We typically recommend that our clients take two weeks at a stretch, and more if they can. It takes at least one week for your body to settle into being on vacation and for the stress level to drop. The second week of a two-week vacation is where you receive the most benefits. We believe that for the entrepreneur in you to thrive, you must have downtime, away from the technical aspects of your practice, to refresh your perspective.

This all-important time away from the firm creates breakthroughs in the way you think about and run your practice. It is this kind of thinking that allows you to create the life and practice you envisioned for yourself at the beginning of this book. Do this to take care of your own well-being as well as that of your practice. You'll be glad you did.

Index

D

F

I

P

R

S

T

V